Introduction to
UK and USA
Culture

김지나 (Gina Kim)
Valerie Hamer

도서출판 동인

Introduction to UK and USA Culture

초　판 ｜ 2016년 2월 28일
저　자 ｜ 김지나, Valerie Hamer
발행인 ｜ 이성모
발행처 ｜ 도서출판 동인
　　　　등록 • 제1-1599호 / 서울시 종로구 명륜동 2가 237 아남주상복A합 118호
　　　　TEL • (02)765-7145 / FAX • (02)765-7165
　　　　E-mail • dongin60@cholian.net / Homepage • donginbook.co.kr

ISBN　978-89-5506-696-8 13740
정　가　15,000원

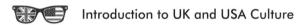 Introduction to UK and USA Culture

Preface

지금은 대학에서 영어를 가르치고 있지만 삼십 여 년 전에 내가 외국인 공포증이 있었다는 사실을 아는 자는 많지 않다. 1983년에 아버지께서 영국으로 유학을 가셨기에 온 가족이 영국 스코틀랜드로 갔을 당시 내가 아는 영어라고는 '헬로, 빠이빠이, 몽키, 바나나' 뿐이었으며 문화적인 사전준비가 없는 상태였으므로 어쩌면 10살인 당시의 나에게 외국인 공포증이 생기는 것이 당연한지도 모르겠다.

세계화가 가속화되는 이 시대에 타문화, 특히 영미문화에 대한 이해는 필수적이다. 충분한 준비 없이 다른 문화와 접촉을 할 경우에 '문화충격'을 피할 수 없고 문화적인 차이로 인한 의사소통 장애가 생기기 마련이다. 2013년부터 대학에서 『영미문화』라는 교과목을 담당하면서 교재를 선정하기 위해 국내, 국외의 서적 및 자료들을 조사해보았으며 2013년부터 3년간 대학 새내기들을 대상으로 영미문화에 대해 지도하면서 영미문화에 관한 책을 집필에 대한 필요성을 더 느끼게 되었다. 영국과 미국 문화에 대한 수많은 영역중에서도 한국인 독자들에게 가장 필요하고 흥미로운 주제인 언어, 가족, 기념일과 축제, 음식, 교육, 여가, 직업, 그리고 혁신분야 위주로 집필하는 과정에서 여러 참고문헌 및 사이트들을 찾았으며 난이도 조절을 위해 개작 및 수정작업을 거쳤다. 문화를 이해하는데 있어서 '영어'의 중요성을 강조해야 하기에 영어로 집필하였다. 혹시 추후에 기회가 되면 역사, 예술, 등 이번 책으로 다루지 못한 분야에 대해서도 조사를 해보고 싶다.

밋밋한 원고가 멋진 책으로 완성되기까지 수고해주신 동인의 이성모 사장님과 편집팀에게 감사를 드린다. 아무쪼록 영미문화에 대해 학생들을 지도하셔야 하는 선생님들에게 도움이 되는 자료가 되길 바란다. 아울러 이 책을 영어와 관련된 전공을 하거나 영어권으로 유학이나 어학연수를 준비하는 학생들, 또는 영미권을 상대로 사업을 하거나 할 계획이 있는 분들에게 추천을 하고 싶다.

2016년 1월
저자 김지나

Introduction to UK and USA Culture

The idea for this book grew from necessity - as we both taught modules on UK - US culture to students who don't have English as their first language, but couldn't find a textbook suitable for use in class. The few available were either aimed at high level EFL students or were out of date, which led us to produce our own material for the courses we ran.

An Introduction to UK and US Culture is designed to be both teacher and student friendly. While the main target audience would be English as a Second/Foreign Language (ESL/EFL) students between high elementary and intermediate level, the content can be adapted to suit students who fall outside of these ranges.

Each unit introduces students to a key aspect of culture, such as language, employment, food and education, covering both UK and US aspects of the topic through facts, figures, readings, a range of activities to suit all learning types, and video clips, where appropriate.

The contents include both supplementary and extension activities, and handy tips for teachers who have access to multi-media resources in the classroom.

Introduction to UK and US Culture is suitable for both key and elective introductory culture courses, and can be adapted to both short and semester long programs.

Val Hamer

CONTENTS

INTRODUCTION 1

What is 'culture'?

- Think about the term: 'culture'
- Are you born with your culture?
- Is it something you learn?

<**The definition of culture** >
(according to Longman's Dictionary of English)

1) The customs, beliefs, art, music and all the other products of human thought made by a particular group of people at a particular time

2) Artistic or other activity of the mind and the works produced by this

* Can you look up other definitions?

Q. When you think of America or Great Britain what image comes to mind?

Q. What are other names for the two countries?

Q. How many states are there in America?

Q. Great Britain is made up of four countries. What are they?

Q. What is American culture? What is British culture?

Tower Bridge, London, UK

Oakland Bay Bridge, San Francisco, USA

THEORY

Below are some scholar's thoughts on culture.

Ting-Toomey (1999)'s the functions of culture:

1) Identity meaning

2) Group inclusion

3) Intergroup boundary regulation

4) Ecological adaptation

5) Culture communication

Dodd (1977)'s relationship between culture and communication;

1) Culture is not genetic.

2) Culture is not learned by individual experience alone but socially.

3) Culture incorporates tradition handed down intergenerationally.

4) Culture involves symbol and code systems which are mediated by man's thought, perceived reality, senses, and social relationships.

5) Language is the means of transmission.

6) Communication is a concomitant part of culture.

7) Communication is both an antecedent and necessary process for intercultural and intercultural relationships.

8) Communication involves both message and channels, that is, the message content with its linguistic components and its symbolic relations and the networks of transmission of information.

9) Cultural communication differentially involves configurational, linear, and configurational-lineral modes of thought.

Ting-Toomey(1999)'s TCC(Transcultural Communication Competence)

Elements:
Tolerance for ambiguity
Open-mindedness
Flexibility
Respectfulness
Adaptation
Sensibility
Creativity

Pesola (1991)- What should be included in 'Culture Education'?

1) Cultural Symbols

1. Flags, insignia related to kid's interests
2. Significant national or geographic monuments
3. Symbols related with holidays
4. Symbols of good and bad luck
5. Symbolic meaning of animals
6. Heroes from history or myth

2) Cultural Products

1. Significant examples of the visual arts and artists
2. Significant examples of the musical arts and composers
3. Important characters, event, and themes from folk literature
4. Traditional children's songs, rhymes, and games
5. Traditional stories and legends
6. Examples of folk art
7. Currency and coins, stamps, and other realia
8. Traditional and holiday foods

3) Cultural Practices

1. Forms of greetings
2. Celebration of holidays
3. Use of gestures
4. Meals and eating practices
5. Shopping
6. Favorite playtime and recreational activities
7. Home and school life
8. Patterns of politeness
9. Types of pets and attitudes toward pets
10. How people move from place to place

Discussion Questions

- What are the elements of culture?
- What should be taught to students regarding American Culture?
- What should be taught to students regarding British Culture?
- What should be taught about other cultures?
- Why is education on culture important?

Maslow's Hierarchy of Needs

(http://cdn-1.simplypsychology.org/maslow-needs.jpg)

Maslow believed that we must fully meet our essential needs (air, food, water, shelter, warmth, sleep and sex) before we can do anything else.

Do you agree?

FACTS

Information on Customs and Etiquette in the U.S.A

Meeting and Greeting

- Greetings are casual.
- A handshake, a smile, and a 'hello' are all that is needed.
- Smile!
- Use first names, and be sure to introduce everyone to each other.
- Say "thank you", "I am sorry" frequently.

Gift Giving Etiquette

- In general, Americans give gifts for birthdays, anniversaries and major holidays, such as Christmas.
- A gift can be as simple as a card and personal note to something more elaborate for a person with whom you are close.
- Gift giving is not an elaborate event, except at Christmas.
- When invited to someone's home for dinner, it is polite to bring a small box of good chocolates, a bottle of wine, a potted plant or flowers for the hostess.
- Gifts are normally opened when received.

Dining Etiquette

- Americans socialize in their homes and 'backyards', in restaurants and in other public places.
  It's not at all unusual for social events to be as casual as a backyard barbecue or a picnic in the park.
- Arrive on time if invited for dinner; no more than 10 minutes later than invited to a small gathering. If it is a large party, it is acceptable to arrive up to 30 minutes later than invited.
- Table manners are more relaxed in the U.S. than in many other countries.
- The fork is held in the right hand and is used for eating. The fork is held tines down. The knife is used to cut or spread something. To use the knife, the fork is switched to the left hand. To continue eating, the fork is switched back to the right hand.

- If you have not finished eating, cross your knife and fork on your plate with the fork over the knife. Indicate you have finished eating by laying your knife and fork parallel across the right side of your plate.
- If you are more comfortable eating in the Continental manner, go ahead. It will not offend anyone.
- Feel free to refuse specific foods or drinks without offering an explanation.
- Many foods are eaten by hand.
- Food is often served family-style, which means that it is in large serving dishes and passed around the table for everyone to serve themselves.
- Do not begin eating until the hostess starts or says to begin.
- Remain standing until invited to sit down.
- Do not rest your elbows on the table.
- Put your napkin in your lap as soon as you sit down.
- Leave a small amount of food on your plate when you have finished eating.

Q. How is this different from your culture?

Stereotypes

What are stereotypes? What role do they play in society?

Stereotypes provide explanations for things that we don't generally have time to think about in detail. They can be problematic because they represent both general and fixed ideas.

It's quite easy to test this by thinking about stereotypes of nationalities.

Task - you can do this together in class in small groups and/or try sending text messages to 5 people in your phone book. The question you need to ask or answer is: what do you think of first in relation to a) an American/America and b) The UK/a Briton?

If you compare answers between groups and with text responses the chances are you will have lots of stereotypical responses.

Stereotypes can also be about class. See the pictures of the lower class and middle class men and women below.

| Stereotypical UK lower working class man | Stereotypical UK lower working class woman | Stereotypical UK middle class man | Stereotypical UK middle class woman |

http://i.telegraph.co.uk/ multimedia/archive/03121/Ben-Thornberry_hig_3121548b.jpg

http://i.dailymail.co.uk/i/ pix/2011/06/05/article-1394469-051CACF10000044D-25_306x434.jpg

http://money.cnn.com/2006/04/10/ news/companies/lehmanintro_f500_ fortune_041706/dick_fuld.03.jpg

http://i.telegraph.co.uk/multimedia/ archive/03396/judge_marilyn_ morn_3396018b.jpg

You may want to think more about this topic through video clips and website links (see 'A Note for the Teacher').

READING

South Korea is becoming more multicultural

Vocabulary Activity for Reading

Can you match these key words and phrases with their meanings?

a. The displaced	1. Individual, not seen elsewhere
b. Oppose	2. Slow progress compared to another thing
c. Unique	3. Those with no home country or place
d. Denied	4. Left out of something
e. Exclusion	5. Don't agree with, hold opposite view to
f. Outpaced	6. Not allowed or given permission to do Something
g. Assimilation	7. Becoming the same as everyone else

In the 21st century borders between countries are becoming more fluid, leading to a growth in multicultural societies.

Global mobility can be caused by:

- People looking for work, or better paid work
- Those looking for adventure in a new and unfamiliar land
- **The displaced** (refugees, asylum seekers)
- People who marry outside of their home nation

However, even though this is becoming more common not all citizens of every country like it. In fact some people actively **oppose** it, often because they think global migration – and inter-cultural marriage weakens their country's **unique** identity. People who feel strongly about this usually also see themselves as a true citizen, and others as guests – of less importance.

If enough people feel this way the experiences of global migrants will not be very good. You can see the results in stories about how refugees running from war have to live – often with no real housing and little food, privacy or comfort.

In Korea it can be seen through the treatment of 4D workers from less developed countries – the people who work dirty and low paid job for long hours. Or by how some foreign English teachers are treated – with job insecurity and low salaries; and many are **denied** health or pension benefits.

Women from poorer countries who marry Korean men often experience this **exclusion** from regular culture too.

It can be difficult for a country like South Korea, which has traditionally been quite isolated from the rest of the world, to know what to do with foreign migrants who move to the country to live, work and get married.

Under these circumstances, since 1995, the number of Korean men who married foreign women has outpaced that of Korean women who married foreign men. IN a demographic sense, Korean society has been rapidly changing in to a multicultural society, but with few cultural preparations.

When we view culture as a narrow set of beliefs and guides to how we should live this masks the experiences of those not born into it, making it more difficult to understand how some groups are excluded. [Even some Koreans can experience this if their lives don't fit exactly into cultural expectations – seniors with no family to take care of them, women who have children outside of marriage, the homeless, and so on.]

The example of poor, foreign Asian women who marry Korean men

Foreign brides have often suffered after marriage, being treated like a slave to a husband and his family. They are usually forced to spend years living as a 'foreign national', being sponsored for a visa which limits her rights, and means she is not independent, even though she plans to live in Korea forever, and has half Korean blood children.

It can take years to reach the goal of full Korean citizenship – the status which offers you true legal protection, and the right to live independently. Meanwhile she must attend a course where she'll be taught Korean language and Korean culture – not to help her enjoy her life here as an individual, but to teach her how to be a good wife and mother to true Korean citizens, (her husband and children.)

Can/should Korea change? Confucian rules favor men in all things, and the men they favor don't seem to want to change anything at all – and why would they? They fail to understand at every level that multiculturalism does not mean **assimilation**. Until laws granting every resident of Korea the right to freedom of movement, and equality - regardless of gender or nationality are respected and upheld there will be no progress.

(Source: adapted from: Advanced English Reading II. Adapted from New Citizens and Multiculturalism in Korea by Youngok Kim)

Reading Comprehension

True or false?

The author:

1. Thinks Korea is becoming a more multicultural society.   T/F
2. Claims that non-Koreans have less rights than Korean citizens.   T/F
3. Believes (Asian) foreign wives are rarely considered full citizens. T/F
4. Says that the influence of Confucianism stops Korea developing fully.   T/F
5. Thinks Korean society has not prepared itself for the changes a
   multicultural society needs to make.   T/F

Compare and discuss your answers with others in the class

General questions

According to the author, what do married migrant women in Korea truly need?
● Do you agree with the author's views?
● Should foreigners who move to another country work hard to become the same as the host country's people?

LANGUAGE 2

INTRODUCTION

Our language skills are one of the key things which set us apart from/above other living creatures. Human beings have developed language beyond the limited set of noises which other animals still use for basic survival, e.g. to warn of danger or tell others about a food supply. Humans are now able to use language in a sophisticated way. drawing on vocabulary, grammar and tone to convey meaning and express feelings.

In many cultures language is now the principal method of communication, whether in written or spoken form, and the way we use it says a lot about who we are, as language and culture have many close connections.

In the US and the UK it is often possible to identify someone's

- age
- gender
- ethnicity
- social class
- location
- educational background

simply by paying attention to the range of language they use.

Language can also be used to create an exclusive circle of knowledge which excludes those unfamiliar with it, e.g. medical or legal speak, or by creating a society where only the rich (or only rich men) learned to read and write.

THEORY

What are the differences between British English and American English?

Talk to another student or make a small group and identify as many things as you can think of without looking at the book or the Internet.

Next we will look at some of the main differences, and you can check how many you identified.

Some differences between US and UK English

1. Spelling
- Suffixes: the tendency is for simplification
    e.g. –ce/-se: defence/defense, practice/practise
- ise/ize: civilise/civilize, organise/organize
- our/-or: colour/color, humour/humor
- Simplification of diphongs (ae, oe) by removal of first letter
    e.g. encyclopaedia/encyclopedia, foetus/fetus
- Double or single "l"
    e.g. counsellor/counselor, marvelous/marvelous

2. Omission of hyphens
e.g. long-time/longtime, pre-teen/preteen

3. General spelling variants
e.g. aluminium/aluminum, cheque/check

4. Word and phrase differences
e.g. autumn/fall, estate agent/realtor

(Read "The Story of English" by Philip Gooden for more information)

\<Considered proper British English\>
-court (not courtroom or courthouse 법원)
-district (not neighborhood 지역)
-normality (not normalcy 정상 상태)
-property (not real estate 부동산)
-stocks (not inventories 재고)

\<Considered old-fashioned terms in Britain\>
- apparel / garment ▶ clothes / clothing
- physicians ▶ doctors
- attorneys ▶ lawyers
- oftentimes ▶ often
- overly ▶ over
- cane ▶ stick
- frock ▶ dress

(Read "That's not English" by Erin Moore for more information)

Shakespeare's Globe, UK

FACTS

History of the English Language

Vocabulary: Key words and phrases

British Empire – foreign countries ruled/governed by the UK e.g. Canada, India etc
Germanic tribes – groups of people from the region which is now Germany/Denmark
Standardization – same each time e.g. McDonalds fries
The dialect of London – the language used in London
Industrial Revolution – the period when factories took over from farming

A short history of the origins and development of English

The history of the English language really started with the arrival of three Germanic tribes who invaded Britain during the 5th century AD. These tribes, the Angles, the Saxons and the Jutes, crossed the North Sea from what today is Denmark and northern Germany.

At that time the inhabitants of Britain spoke a Celtic language, but most of the Celtic speakers were pushed west and north by the invaders - mainly into what is now Wales, Scotland and Ireland. The Angles came from "Englaland" [sic] and their language was called "Englisc" - from which the words "England" and "English" are derived.

- **Old English** (450-1100 AD)
  The invading Germanic tribes spoke similar languages, which in Britain developed into what we now call Old English. Old English did not sound or look like English today. Native English speakers now would have great difficulty understanding Old English. Nevertheless, about half of the most commonly used words in Modern English have Old English roots. The words 'be', 'strong' and 'water', for example, derive from Old English. Old English was spoken until around 1100.

- **Middle English** (1100-1500)
  In 1066 William the Conqueror, the Duke of Normandy (part of modern France), invaded and conquered (took over) England. The new conquerors (called the Normans) brought with them a kind of French, which became the language of the Royal Court, and the ruling and business classes.

For some time there was a class division, as the lower classes/poor people spoke English and the upper classes/rich and ruling people spoke French. In the 14th century English became dominant in Britain again, but with many French words added. This language is called Middle English.
It was the language of the great poet Chaucer (c1340-1400), but it would still be difficult for native English speakers to understand today.

- **Early Modern English** (1500-1800)
Towards the end of Middle English, the way English was pronounced, (called the Great Vowel Shift), started, with vowels being pronounced shorter and shorter. Then, from the 16th century the British people had contact with many people from around the world, and new words and phrases entered the language.
The invention of printing also meant that there was now a common language in print. Books became cheaper and more people learned to read. Printing also brought **standardization** to English. Spelling and grammar became fixed, and **the dialect of London**, where most publishing houses were, became the standard. In 1604 the first English dictionary was published.

- **Late Modern English** (1800-Present)
The main difference between Early Modern English and Late Modern English is vocabulary. Late Modern English has many more words, for two main reasons – the **Industrial Revolution** and technology created a need for new words, and **the British Empire** covered one quarter of the earth's surface, and the English language adopted foreign words from many countries.

(Source: https://www.englishclub.com/english-language-history.htm)

READING

American English vs. British English

- American English is the form of English used in the United States. It includes all English dialects used within the United States of America.
- British English is the form of English used in the United Kingdom. It includes all English dialects used within the United Kingdom.
- Differences between American and British English include pronunciation, grammar, vocabulary (lexis), spelling, punctuation, idioms, and formatting of dates and numbers.

Comparison chart

	American English	British English
Pronunciation differences	Some words pronounced differently in the languages are Methane, Interpol	Some words pronounced differently in the languages are Methane, Interpol
Spelling differences	flavor, honor, analyze, color etc.	flavour, honour, analyse, colour etc.
Title differences	Mr., Mrs.	Mr, Mrs
Different meanings	wash up (=your face, body)	wash up (=the dishes)
What is it?	American English is the form of English used in the United States. It includes all English dialects used within the United States of America.	British English is the form of English used in the United Kingdom. It includes all English dialects used within the United Kingdom. It is also used in Ireland, Australia, New Zealand, Canada and other Commonwealth regions.

History of British vs. American English

The English language was introduced to America through British colonization in the early 17th century. It also spread to many other parts of the world because of the strength of the British empire. Over the years, English spoken in the United States and in Britain started diverging from each other in various aspects. This led to new dialects in the form of American English.

① Differences in Accents

Prior to the Revolutionary War and American independence from the British in 1776, American and British accents were similar. Both were rhotic i.e. speakers pronounced the letter R in hard. Since 1776 the accents diverged, but the English accent in America has changed less drastically than accents in Britain.

Towards the end of the 18th century non-rhotic speech took off in southern England, especially among the upper classes; this "prestige" non-rhotic speech was standardized, and has been spreading in Britain ever since.

Most American accents, however, remained rhotic.

There are a few fascinating exceptions: New York and New England accents became non-rhotic, perhaps because of the region's British connections. Irish and Scottish accents, however, remained rhotic.

To be fair, both American and British English have several types of accents and there is no one true American or British accent.

② Differences in use of Tenses

In British English the present perfect is used to express an action that has occurred in the recent past that has an effect on the present moment. For example: I've misplaced my pen. Can you help me find it? In American English, the use of the past tense is also permissible: I misplaced my pen. Can you help me find it? In British English, however, using the past tense in this example would be considered incorrect.

Other differences involving the use of the present perfect in British English and simple past in American English include the words already, just and yet.

British English: I've just had food. Have you finished your homework yet? American English: I just had food. OR I've just had food.

I've already seen that film. OR I already saw that film.

③ Differences in Vocabulary

While some words may mean something in British English, the same word might be something else in American English and vice versa. For example, 'athlete' in British English is one who participates in track and field events whereas 'athlete' in American English is one who participates in sports in general.

Rubber in British English: tool to erase pencil markings.

Rubber in American English: condom.

There are also some words like AC, Airplane, bro, catsup, cell phone etc. which are common in American English and not used very often in British English. Some words widely used in British English and seldom in American English are advert, anti clockwise, barrister, cat's eye.

④ Differences in Spelling

There are many words that are spelt differently in both forms of English. Some examples are:

American English spelling	British English spelling
color	colour
fulfill	fulfil
center	centre
analyze	analyse
aging	ageing
dialog	dialogue
anesthesia	anaesthesia

⑤ Differences in the use of Prepositions

There are also a few differences between British and American English in the use of prepositions. For example: while the British would play in a team, Americans would play on a team. Another example: while the British would go out at the weekend, Americans would go out on the weekend.

⑥ Differences in Verb usage

American and British English may also use a base verb in different manners. For example: For the verb "to dream", Americans would use the past tense dreamed, while the British would use dreamt in past tense. The same applies to "learned" and "learnt". Another example of differing past tense spellings for verbs in American and British English is "forecast". Americans use forecast while the British would say forecasted in simple past tense.

⑦ Differences in Pronunciation

Some words that are pronounced differently in American vs. British English are controversy, leisure, schedule etc. There are also some words like Ax (Axe in British) and Defense (Defence in British) which have the same pronunciation but different spellings in both languages.

⑧ Time telling in British vs. American English

Both languages have a slightly different structure of telling the time. While the British would say quarter past ten to denote 10:15, it is not uncommon in America to say quarter after or even a quarter after ten.

Thirty minutes after the hour is commonly called half past in both languages. Americans always write digital times with a colon, thus 6:00, whereas Britons often use a point, 6.00.

⑨ Differences in Punctuation

While the British would write Mr, Mrs, Dr, the Americans would write Mr., Mrs., Dr.

(Source: http://www.diffen.com/difference/American_English_vs_British_English)

Questions for students

1. Which style of English is most common/popular in your country?
2. Which do you think is most important, and why?
3. What % of the world do you think learns and uses US or UK English? Compare your ideas with another student or a group.

The map below covers countries with British English as a main or second official language.

(Credit: https://upload.wikimedia.org/wikipedia/commons/2/26/The_British_Empire.png)

Of course not all of these countries use or speak English the way people in the UK today do. Over time they are adapted and changed.

Learn more by looking online for terms such as : Singlish
This is a good site for more information on this topic.
https://www.pinterest.com/pin/21673641930089722/

Activity 1: UK English 'slang' – which meaning is correct?

- Make a pair with another student. Decide who is student 1 and student 2. Student 1 starts – read a word and the three clues. Mark the answer your partner thinks is correct. Then student 2 asks.
- When you are both finished look at the answers in the final section of this book.

Student 1

Give you a bell	a) Wave to you	b) Call you	c) Ignore you
Gutted	a) Devastated	b) Sick	c) Angry
Chuffed	a) Hungry	b) Proud	c) Tired
Lost the Plot	a) Gone Crazy	b) Can't find your way	c) Lost your key
Sorted	a) Tidy up	b) Change plan	c) Arranged
Kip	a) Hurt someone	b) Sleep or nap	c) Eat a snack
Bee's Knees	a) Awesome	b) Honey	c) Catch a bug
Dodgy	a) Avoid someone	b) Loan cash	c) Suspicious

Student 2

Wonky	a) Happy	b) Clever	c) Not right
Skive	a) Tease	b) Avoid doing something	c) Sleep
Toff	a) Candy	b) Upper class	c) Sticky
Starkers	a) Naked	b) Story	c) Late
Loo	a) Kitchen	b) Toilet	c) Bedroom
Nicked	a) Winner	b) Late	c) Stolen
Gobsmacked	a) Angry	b) Trouble maker	c) Amazed
Bog Roll	a) Toilet Paper	b) Cake	c) Exercise

Activity 2: Match the correct American English word to its British English equivalent.

	Korean	British English	American English
1	승강기	Lift	
2	우편	Post	
3	감자칩	Chips	
4	감자튀김	Crisps	
5	반창고	Plasters	
6	운동화	Trainers	
7	쿠키	Biscuits	
8	약국	Chemist's shop	
9	축구	Football	
10	미식축구	American football	
11	트렁크	Trunk	
12	스웨터	Jumper	
13	기름(차량용)	Petrol	
14	주차장	Car park	
15	핸드폰	Mobile phone	
16	지하철	Underground/Tube	
17	인도	Pavement	
18	1층	Ground floor/Lobby	
19	손전등	Torch	
20	아파트	Flat	
21	사탕	Sweets	
22	가을	Autumn	
23	술집	Pub	
24	쓰레기통	Bin	
25	냅킨	Serviette	

American English words

Candy   Parking   Soccer   Bar   Trash can   Cell phone   Napkin   Football   Fries
Mail   Sweater   Band aid   Subway   Fall   Flash light   Apartment   First floor   Chips
Elevator   Sneakers   Cookies   Gas   Trunk   Sidewalk   Pharmacy/drug store

THE FAMILY

INTRODUCTION

1. How would you explain the term 'the family' to someone who didn't know it?

2. Compare your answer to the above question with what your classmates have written. Are they the same or different?

3. Now use a dictionary (paper or online) to look for the meaning of family, and write the first definition you find here:

4. Is the dictionary definition similar to your own answer in #1? If not, note the differences below.

The family is an important part of life in most cultures, but the way we define what a family is and how it works is not always the same.

Families can be formed differently and play different roles:
- between countries
- within a country

And of course the idea of what a family is also changes through time.

In the UK and the USA the concept of family is very fluid, and these days it is impossible to define what a 'typical family' is in those countries.

\<Types of family units in 21st century UK/USA\>

Nuclear family (also called conjugal, elementary, traditional or immediate family)	Father, mother and children
Extended family	Nuclear style family + family from other generations (or cousins, siblings)
Blended (or reconstituted) family	Parents and children from this and previous relationships
Single parent family	Either mother or father and one or more children
Astronaut family (new term)	One parent lives/works in another country
Child free families	A married couple who have no children
Same-sex families	Two parents of the same gender and their children

Q. Do you know people who live in these types of families?

FACTS

Take a look at these words. You will see them again when reading some facts about the family in UK & USA.

A half century	fifty years
Milestones	major points in life e.g. becoming an adult, marriage
Spouse	husband or wife
Hispanic	generally used to refer to people from South and Central America
Infant	a baby or very young child

General Facts

- Most people will live in several types of family structures during their life.
- Immigrants have changed the definition of what was considered 'typical'.

- These days people are more likely to marry someone from a different ethnic, racial, religious or political background to themselves.
- 58% of couples who marry in the UK today will never get a divorce.
- In the UK, women aged 25-29 are twice as likely to get divorced as any other age group.
- These days people get married later than ever. In 1990, 23 was the average age for a woman to marry in the UK or the US.
- The average UK woman marries at age 28.9 years, for men this is 30.8 years. (Compared to 27 and 29 for US citizens.)
- The average American married couple spend just 4 minutes alone together from waking up to going to bed.
- Love has only been connected to marriage for a few hundred years. Before that most people married to secure property and inheritance lines, or to create powerful friends. Even poor people married just to make babies so they could have workers for their land.

Facts about the modern American family

1. Americans are putting off life's big milestones. Today, the average age for a first marriage is 29 for men and 27 for women—the highest in modern history.
   - In 1960 - 65% of Americans aged between 18 – 32 were married. In 2013 – only 26% were. Women are also waiting longer to have children.
   - In 1960 – 40% of mothers were aged between 15-24 years. In 2011 this number was only 22%.

2. Today, the average American woman will have 1.9 children.
   - In 1960, this figure was 3.7 children.

3. Families today come in many forms. (refer to the table in the introduction section) 44% of young people ages 18 to 29 have a step sibling. Compare this to people over 65 years – only 16% of that group have a step sibling.

4. More babies are born to unmarried mothers than ever before.
   - In 1960 around 5% of babies were born to unmarried women.
   - In 2011 – 41% were. (71% of births to black women, 29% for white women)
   - Women with a university degree less likely to have a baby while unmarried (9%).

5. Intermarriage among people of different races is increasingly common.
- In 1980, just 7% of all marriages in the U.S. were between spouses of a different race/ethnicity.
- In 2010, that share has doubled to 15% of all new marriages in the U.S.
  Hispanics (26%) and Asians (28%) were most likely to "marry out," compared with 9% of whites and 17% of blacks.

(Adapted from www.pewresearch.org/fact-tank/2014/04/30/5-facts-about-the-modern-american-family/

T/F Activity on Facts

True/False – use the facts above to decide if each statement is true or false.
1. Modern Americans are marrying at a later age than has ever been recorded in history. T/F
2. In 1960, 40% of all mothers with small children were aged under 24 years. T/F
3. A modern American woman will probably only have one child. T/F
4. Younger Americans are much more likely to have a step-sibling than older Americans. T/F
5. Marriage between people from different ethnic backgrounds is much more common now. T/F

Discussion Activity on Facts

Work in a pair or a small group and answer/talk about the following questions.

1. The writer claims that in modern America only 16% of families are made up of two married people raising their own children.

   * How does this compare to families in your country?

   * Is the 16% figure a shock to you? Why, or why not?

   * Do you think families work better when they follow this traditional (man and woman, married) model? Why?

2. How many children do people have, on average, in your country?

   * Is this the same number as American women? If not, why?

   * Why do you think American women are having fewer children?

   * Should women have more children? Why? If yes, how could you persuade them to?

STATISTICS

In 1960, 37% of homes included married parents raising only their own children. These days just 16% of households look like that.

UK/2014/Gov stats

In 2014 there were 18.6 million families.

- 12.5 million married couple families (11% of these are blended type)
- 2 million single parents (91% of these being women)
- The others are cohabiting
  (Same sex couples will be recorded and reported as a unique category in the next census)

The UK had 26.7 million households, a quarter of them featured just one person.

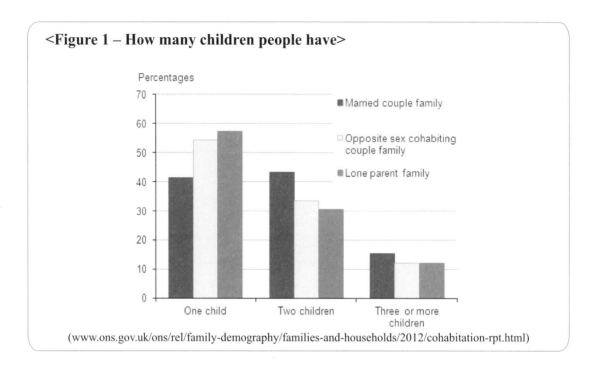

<Figure 1 – How many children people have>

Percentages

- ■ Married couple family
- □ Opposite sex cohabiting couple family
- ■ Lone parent family

(www.ons.gov.uk/ons/rel/family-demography/families-and-households/2012/cohabitation-rpt.html)

Q. Who has the most children?

Q. What do these statistics tell us about families?

< Figure 2 - Birthrates in the USA>

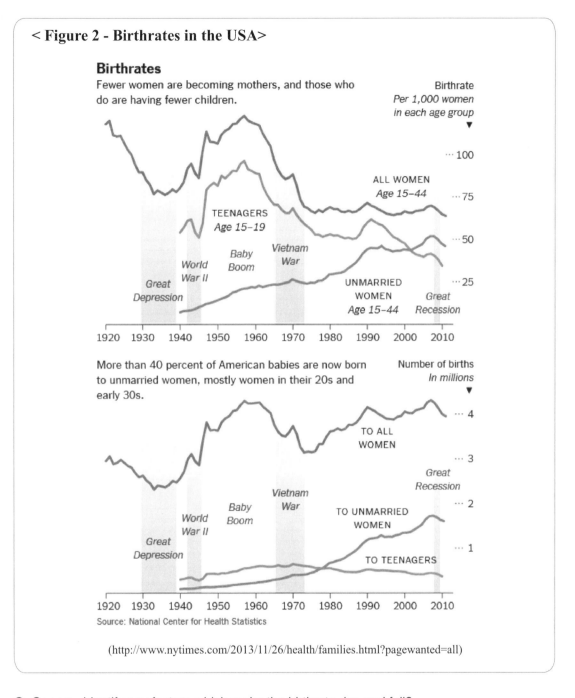

Birthrates

Fewer women are becoming mothers, and those who do are having fewer children.

Birthrate
Per 1,000 women
in each age group
▼

ALL WOMEN
Age 15–44

TEENAGERS
Age 15–19

Baby Boom

Vietnam War

World War II

Great Depression

UNMARRIED WOMEN
Age 15–44

Great Recession

··· 100
···75
···50
···25

1920 1930 1940 1950 1960 1970 1980 1990 2000 2010

More than 40 percent of American babies are now born to unmarried women, mostly women in their 20s and early 30s.

Number of births
In millions
▼

TO ALL WOMEN

Great Recession

Vietnam War

Baby Boom

World War II

Great Depression

TO UNMARRIED WOMEN

TO TEENAGERS

··· 4
··· 3
··· 2
··· 1

1920 1930 1940 1950 1960 1970 1980 1990 2000 2010

Source: National Center for Health Statistics

(http://www.nytimes.com/2013/11/26/health/families.html?pagewanted=all)

Q. Can you identify any factors which make the birthrate rise and fall?

Q. What do the charts tell us about the changing patterns of child bearing?

<Figure 3 – Marriage and Divorce>

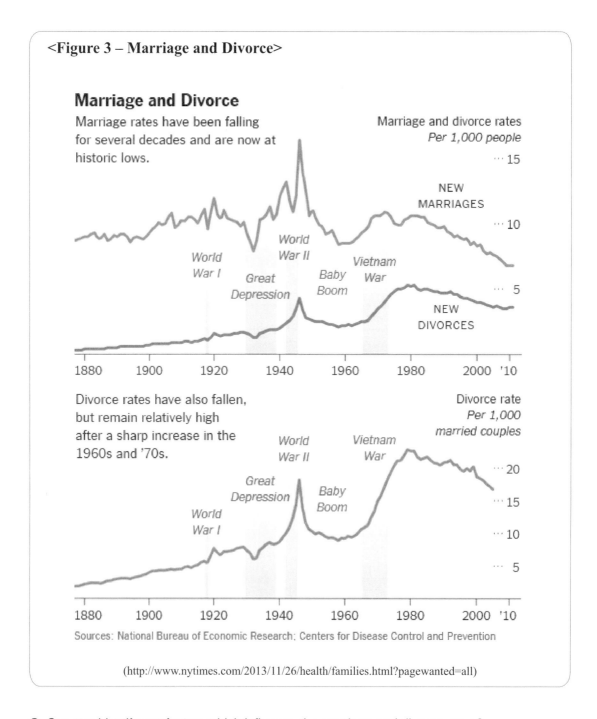

Marriage and Divorce

Marriage rates have been falling for several decades and are now at historic lows.

Marriage and divorce rates
Per 1,000 people

Divorce rates have also fallen, but remain relatively high after a sharp increase in the 1960s and '70s.

Divorce rate
Per 1,000 married couples

Sources: National Bureau of Economic Research; Centers for Disease Control and Prevention

(http://www.nytimes.com/2013/11/26/health/families.html?pagewanted=all)

Q. Can you identify any factors which influence the marriage and divorce rates?

Q. What do the charts tell us about the changing patterns of marriage and divorce?

THEORY

Theorists explain the reason we live in family units in different ways. This is why there is no one answer to questions like: What role does the family play in society and culture?

There are many different theories with different explanations, but here we just look at 3 of the major perspectives.

1. Functionalism (right wing)

IN BRIEF - basically the traditional family structure is essential for a stable society. With a father to work outside the house the mother takes care of the domestic duties which sustain his efforts, and educates the next generation to do the same.

The family, a group of people living in legally acknowledged private units, keeps society stable. This happens because when living this way the family:

- Socialises children (parents, older siblings and other family members who live there teach younger members how to behave).
- Controls sexual behaviour and reproduction. (Two people in a sexually exclusive relationship will have fewer children, which means those they have will be better provided for.)
- Each family member inherits a 'social identity' (which means they will have the social class position, religion, ethnic background of their parents. This puts them into a pecking order in society.)
- Is a constant and free source of practical and emotional support (love, encouragement, food, clothing, shelter)

The family must be protected as if it is changed or threatened society could crumble. Men are breadwinners, women manage the domestic arena, providing stability. Children will suffer if this changes. ANY other type of family setup will damage them.

Everybody has a place in society, and plays a role. (Social stratification). Not all are equal, that would be impossible, but they are all needed to keep society running smoothly, and the family must teach children to accept this.

2. Conflict (Left wing)

Conflict theorists agree that the family plays an important role in caring for and socialising children, but believe that there is a dark side to the family, which they think:

- Encourages social inequality – the poor will always be poor.
- Promotes men as the powerful leader, which encourages violence within the home
- Not all families provide emotional support and live happily together. It can be the place of conflict, unhappiness, incest etc.
- Families are promoted as ideal way of living because they guarantee two things.
  1. That money is inherited by legitimate kids.
  2. They produce fodder for factories.
- Teaching children to accept their place means few can advance and change.

3. Feminism

- Feminists are often negative about the family because they see it as a place where men oppress women.
- Women do the housework, even if they have a paid job outside the home.
- Men gain from women's work.
- Children are socialised into perpetuating gender roles, which reinforces the idea that men are superior.
- Female biology is used against them.

READING 1

The Extended Family Today

> **Before you read – let's look at some important vocabulary.**
>
> **Recession** — a weak economy
> **Modest** — not fancy, large or expensive
> **Pitching in** — helping with a task
> **Splits the phone bill** — shares the cost of the phone bill
> **Friction** — tension/arguments
> **Multi-generational households** — children, parents and grandparents living together
>
> *NOW, choose a word or words from the list to fill in the blank*

Donna Tam was a 29-year-old reporter in San Francisco when she moved back into the family home. She now lives with her parents, grandmother and younger brother in a _____ home. Her friends asked if she was trying to save money?

They couldn't understand why she would give up her freedom. "It's definitely crowded, but I think it's what I'm used to. I've been living this way since I was little," said Tam.

Even after the _____ more and more Americans are living with their parents and grandparents to save money. But for many Asian immigrant households, this isn't new.

According to the Pew Research Center, Asians are twice as likely as whites to live in _____ — and considering Asians are also America's fastest-growing ethnic group, this housing trend is here to stay.

For the Tam family, three generations under one roof is a tradition, a duty. Lee Jin Ho is Tam's 93-year-old grandmother. Growing up in China, she lived with her parents and grandparents.

Now, in the US, she lives with her children and helped raise her grandchildren. She would never want to live by herself, she said. She loves living with her family. Donna Tam remembers her grandmother walking her to and from school and making snacks.

When she lived alone Tam usually ate dinner at her parent's house, so eventually, she decided to live where she spent most of her time.

Today, Tam pays rent, _____ with her sister, and gives money to her brother, a college student. Her parents never asked her do any of this, but she knew what was expected.

"In Chinese families, a lot of how we do our day-to-day things is based on [a] 'we're all in it together' kind of thing," Tam said. "There's a lot of _____." Everyone has chores, even Grandma Lee. She maintains the living room's large Buddhist shrine and makes holiday treats.

Tam's brother, Alex, helps Grandma Lee open jars and crush peanuts and gives her rides to the doctor or to restaurants, though she still often walks. Donna Tam helps her mom, who's from Vietnam, if she has questions about something she's reading in English.

But Tam sometimes struggles with her decision to move home. To get to her bedroom, she must pass through her grandmother's room. And there's little privacy.

"These five adults live in a house together, but two of them you know don't see themselves as kids," she said, "and three of them see those two as kids. So there's going to be_____."

What's important is... just keeping in perspective what your parents did for you or what your grandparents did for you. What you can do for the generations that come after you. That's how you, kind of, keep it together."

Adapted from:

www.pri.org/stories/2013-10-14/living-three-generations-house-has-its-benefits-privacy-not-one-them

Comprehension Questions for Reading 1

1. Why did Tam move back into the family home?

2. How many adults live in the house now?

3. Note the advantages and disadvantages she mentions about living with her family.

READING 2

Katie's Story - My Large Family

Before you read

Exercise 1

Ask your partner the following questions. Discuss your answers and reasons with your partner, and then with another pair of students.

- How many people live in your family home?
- Would you like to live in a family with lots of children?

Exercise 2

Match the words and definitions, then compare your answers with someone else in your class.

LIST A	LIST B
Eldest	Stop doing something
Important milestones	Badly organized/too casual/careless
Quit	A person who buys, improves and sells buildings
Flick through	A big event in your life e.g. baby learns to talk
Sloppy	Look through something
Commercial property developer	The oldest

Exercise 3

You are going to read a story about a woman called Katie, and her family.
Before you read the story try to guess what these numbers may describe.
You can do this alone and then share your ideas, or work with a partner from the start.

39 _____

18 months _____

7 _____

3 _____

1999 _____

11 months _____

One and a half days _____

Exercise 4

Now read the article quickly and look for these numbers. Make a note of what they are describing. Were you correct with your guesses?

39 _____

18 months _____

7 _____

3 _____

1999 _____

11 months _____

One and a half days _____

Now read Katie's story

My Large Family

We are a family of two parents (Mum and Dad) and eight children. Our eldest, who is twelve years old, is the only boy. We have seven daughters, the baby is eighteen months old, and one set of twins, who are nearly three.

When I was younger I never imagined I'd have eight children at age 39! I always said I would use my education and have a paid job, even after having children.

After baby number one (born in 1999) was eleven months old I went to work three days a week. We really needed the money and I was bored without adult company all day.

My parents cared for him two days a week, and one day a week he attended childcare. I hadn't expected it to be so difficult to have others care for him, and it made me feel sad when I missed important milestones like his first word, or first step. It was a dilemma. I wanted to be with him, but also to have some independence.
Baby number two was born in 2001 and I dropped to one day at work every week. The next year I had my third child and quit working outside the house for good. I felt happy about this decision, more relaxed than in the past, and I now had a network of friends in the same position.

My husband is a commercial property developer and works flexible hours so he does a lot around the house and with the kids. When I met him I knew he'd be a great father, and that fact was important to me. We are great partners, and always support each other through the bad days.

It's not always easy to live in a very big family but overall we get it right most of the time.

These days we have a nanny help us for one and a half days a week. We hired her to help because my parents, (who help a lot) got sick, and we realised we won't have them around forever. We can't manage without the amazing people who support us by taking care of the children at different times.

Originally I planned to do household jobs such as gardening or cleaning while the nanny took care of the children, but now I use the time to go shopping, take one of the children out for lunch, or meet my husband for a coffee.

Preparing food for ten people takes some planning. I am a great fan of the weekly menu planner. The children generally choose a night each. I encourage the bigger children to flick through cookbooks or use the internet to find something they like.

A planned menu makes shopping easier, and I go to the supermarket once a week, buy fruit and vegetables locally, and bake a sweet treat most afternoons.

I am ALWAYS washing. Everything is dried in the machine, and I stopped ironing after baby number 8.

I think it is important that all the children look nice, and I brush their hair every day. They also shower daily. I don't want people to think we are a big, sloppy family, or for the children to think they are not cared for properly.

Sometimes people say we are lucky to have such a big and lovely family – but I think it's more about hard work and effort than good luck.

Adapted from: http://planningwithkids.com/2011/09/28/our-big-family-story/

Check your Understanding for Reading 2
Choose the correct answer from each set of 3 choices

1. Katie's family type is:
   a) Nuclear
   b) Extended
   c) Blended

2. When she was younger Katie thought she would:
   a) Have lots of children
   b) Have a job which used her knowledge
   c) Have no children

3. Katie's husband:
   a) Is too busy at work to help take care of the children
   b) Can arrange his work around taking care of the children with Katie
   c) Takes care of the children full time

CELEBRATIONS

INTRODUCTION

Answer the following questions with a partner or small group

Which holidays and special days are the most important in your country?

How many global 'special days and holidays' do you know?

The term 'celebrations and special days' includes public/national holidays when many people have a day off work or school, informal special days which many people celebrate but don't have time off for, and special days and times where only one, two or a few people celebrate at one time.

Throughout the world some of these days are shared by the people of many countries, others are unique to only one or two. In this unit you will learn about some of these days, some of them are popular in either the USA or the UK, others in both.

You will also discover more about how the same special day or celebration involves quite different things between the two countries.

Fireworks on July 4, USA

USA Holidays

In the US there are two types of holidays: legal (federal) holidays and traditional holidays

Legal holidays mean that official places such as banks, government offices, post offices, and usually many businesses, close. Of course the emergency services and service workers such as (some) store assistants, or transport operators will not have this day free.

The following are legal American holidays:

- New Year's Day
- Martin Luther King Day
- President's Day
- Memorial Day
- Independence Day
- Labor Day
- Columbus Day
- Veterans Day,
- Thanksgiving
- Christmas
- Inauguration Day, (welcoming a new president) is a legal holiday - once every 4 years

Traditional special days are celebrated for fun, but there is not an official day off work or school.

The most well-known traditional special days in the USA are:

- Valentine's Day
- St. Patrick's Day
- Easter
- April Fools' Day
- Mother's Day
- Flag Day
- Father's Day
- Halloween

UK Holidays

In the UK Easter and Boxing Day (December 26th) are **legal holidays**. There are also more days off work for no special reason, days known simply as 'bank holiday Monday'. While in the USA a lot of legal holidays are celebrating famous people from history, and many are connected to their early struggles to make America a good place to live and the fight for independence from the UK. People in the UK have many of the same **traditional special days** as the USA, although sometimes they are on different dates, or involve different types of celebrations. Some are not known in the USA at all.

Most special days and celebrations have an interesting history, and this is something your teacher may ask you to research on this course. For now let's look at some of the informal special days UK people enjoy.

April Fool's Day

The idea is that on April 1st you can play pranks on people, but only until noon. If you try after that it is bad luck.

Christmas Day

In families with children someone usually gets up very early and puts a large turkey into the oven to cook. It can take several hours. The children will wake early and want to find the presents Santa brought them. They will probably eat chocolate for breakfast!
People often sit together to open their X'mas presents after breakfast.

Mothers often complain they have too much food preparation and cooking to do, especially if a lot of the family come to visit. At around 3pm the queen makes a speech which people watch on TV, and then they eat their special Christmas dinner.

Kids pulling crackers, UK

Traditional Christmas Dinner

After dinner they eat Christmas pudding. People usually eat too much and spend the rest of the afternoon asleep!

Halloween

This special day is becoming more and more like the American style, with trick or treating replacing the traditional routine of children performing a song or dance in order to get a little cash or a few sweets.

Easter

Although people in the UK don't go to church as often as they used to, Easter is still a time when many people will attend a church service. (This is also a 4 day legal holiday, from Good Friday through to Easter Monday.) Many people exchange 'Easter eggs', which are chocolate shaped like an egg, and painting regular eggs is a popular activity at this time.

Pancake Day (Shrove Tuesday)

This is a holiday unique to the UK and some Commonwealth countries; the date changes, depending when Easter falls each year. On this day many people make pancakes (crepes) to use up their eggs, flour and milk before Lent. There are also often special races where people run with a pancake in a frying pan.

Bonfire night

You can learn about this unique UK celebration in the reading section of the book later.

Other holidays

The UK is a multicultural country, so the special days of various religions and cultures are also celebrated, though often just by those involved.

- Ramadam
- Women's Day
- Earth Day
- Remembrance Day
- Winter Solstice

Celebration days/events

Just like legal holidays or traditional special days, there are some celebrations which are popular in both the US and the UK.

These are usually based on one of the following:

Age
- ▶ becoming an adult
- ▶ 'milestone birthdays' - they end in a zero
- ▶ retiring

Marriage
- ▶ engagement
- ▶ hen/stag party
- ▶ wedding

Babies
- ▶ baby showers (another event borrowed from the USA)
- ▶ christening/naming

Key facts

- ♣ Some holidays are celebrated around the world, others are only known in 1-2 countries.
- ♣ Some special days involve only 1 – 2 people, others are for everyone.
- ♣ Some are about religion, some have origins in religion but in modern times not everyone cares   about that.
- ♣ Some are about the world/earth/equality, others are about drinking alcohol!
- ♣ We give presents on some days, but not on others.
- ♣ Some days have special food, others don't.

Q. Are any of these special days celebrated in your country? How? Is it different from the US/ UK?

Q. Are there any special days that you think are only important to your country and culture? What are they?

READING 1

Vocabulary from Reading 1

Check the meanings before you read.

Baked potatoes (jacket potatoes) – large potatoes cooked in an oven or fire with the skin on.

Effigy – a doll or similar that looks like someone

Villain – a bad guy/criminal

Government – the people who make rules about a country

UK – Bonfire Night/Guy Fawkes Night

"Remember, remember the 5th of November." The people of Britain certainly do, and they have every year since 1605!!

That's over 400 years of a huge once a year party that in modern Britain means fireworks, **baked potatoes** and throwing an **effigy** of a long dead **villain** onto huge bonfires. But why?

This is the man who is responsible. His name is Guy Fawkes, and on November 5th 1605 he was part of a group who tried to kill the king (James 1st) and the **government** by blowing up the building they were working in. (The House of Lords).

The plan was discovered before they could hurt anyone, and people lit fires all around the country to celebrate.

The government decided to make November 5th a day to celebrate every year.

These days groups of people often build community bonfires – huge fires which can be 10 or 20 metres high – and then local people can enjoy it together.

In the week before bonfire night many children in the UK will make a 'Guy'. Often they dress an old Teddy bear up, or use a football for a head and old clothes filled with paper for the body.

Many children push the 'Guy' around in a baby's pram, or they stand outside a shop and ask people to give 'a penny for the Guy'.

They can make quite a lot of money!!

A video to watch: www.youtube.com/watch?v=bcyXMLz3fK0

Reading 2

Saint Patrick's Day USA Style

Saint Patrick's Day, or the Feast of Saint Patrick, is a cultural and religious celebration held on 17 March, the traditional death day of Saint Patrick, the patron saint of Ireland.

Saint Patrick was a 5th-century Christian missionary and bishop in Ireland. It is believed that he was born in Roman Britain in the fourth century. His father was a deacon of the Roman Empire.

Patrick said he was kidnapped at age 16 by Irish pirates, where he was forced to work as a shepherd in Ireland for 6 years. During this time he became religious. When he escaped and ran to Britain Patrick studied to become a priest. He lived in France for a while and then returned to Ireland and converted many people to the Catholic faith.

Over the following centuries, many legends grew up around Patrick and he became Ireland's foremost saint. He is remembered for his hard work through celebrations all around the world. Many of these celebrate Irish heritage in general.

There may be public parades public parades and festivals, dances, and green costumes. Christians also attend church services, such as worship or mass, and the Lenten restrictions on eating and drinking alcohol are lifted for the day, which encourages the holiday's tradition of alcohol consumption.

Saint Patrick's Day is a public holiday in the Republic of Ireland, Northern Ireland and a few other places. It is also widely celebrated by people with Irish ancestors around the world, especially in Great Britain, Canada, the United States, Australia, New Zealand, and other countries.

In the United States, Saint Patrick's Day is not a legal holiday at all. Only Suffolk County, Massachusetts and Savannah, Georgia authorized Saint Patrick's Day as a legal holiday. However, the United States also celebrate this as recognition of Irish and American culture.

The holiday has been celebrated on the North American continent since the late eighteen century. At first, in 1737, Boston's Irish Society celebrates Saint Patrick's Day simply to honor its homeland.

Today, Saint Patrick's Day is widely celebrated in America by Irish and non-Irish alike. Seattle and other cities paint the traffic stripe of their parade routs green. Chicago dyes its river green and has done so since 1962 when sewer workers used green dye to check for sewer discharges and had the idea to turn the river green for Saint Patrick's Day. Indianapolis also dyes its main canal green.

Sources: (https://en.wikipedia.org/wiki/Saint_Patrick)
       (https://en.wikipedia.org/w/index.php?title=Saint_Patrick%27s_Day&redirect=no)
       (https://en.wikipedia.org/wiki/Saint_Patrick%27s_Day_in_the_United_States)

Comprehension questions for Reading 2

Answer the questions and then compare your ideas with another student's.

    1. What date is St. Patrick's Day celebrated?

    2. Where and when was St. Patrick said to be born?

    3. Who did Patrick claim kidnapped him at age 16?

    4. Is Saint Patrick's Day a legal holiday in every country of the world?

    5. Which colour is associated with St. Patrick?

    6. Is Saint Patrick's Day celebrated in your country?

HOUSES 5

INTRODUCTION

> **Before you read**
>
> • What kind of housing is more popular in your country, apartments, houses or something else?
> • Do people prefer to live in big cities, large towns or in rural areas?
> • Do most people (want to) buy or rent?

In the introduction unit (Chapter 1) we looked at Maslow's hierarchy of needs. Do you remember that housing (shelter) was considered a basic human need?

Housing is not just about being able to stay warm and dry, although of course that is important. It's also connected to feelings of self worth as it provides privacy from the world and independence. Despite it being so important not everyone in the UK and the USA has access to a place they can call home, and many others live in inadequate conditions.

In general, the housing people in the USA and the UK live in depends on economics, personal lifestyle and cultural rules.

Q. Can you classify the different types of houses shown below? Let's do some researching.

Types	Characteristics
Two Family House	
Town House	
Condominium	
Duplex House	
Semi-detached House	
Co-op	

FACTS & STATISICS – UK

- The UK government sold a lot of public (built and owned by the state, cheaper rents) housing during the 1980s when they let tenants buy them cheaply. Now there are not enough for needy people to live in.
- In the UK most people want to buy a property, unlike other EU countries where renting is the preferred choice.
- Types of houses in the UK
  http://resources.woodlands-junior.kent.sch.uk/customs/questions/houses.htm
- There are about 25 million homes in the UK, of which seven out of 10 are owner-occupied. The number of home owners has risen by more than one million since 1997 alone.
- In 1918, eight out of 10 homes were rented privately, compared with one in 10 now. The number of people in social housing has fallen to fewer than two in 10.
- Home ownership is lowest in London (58%) and Scotland (67%). The majority of single parents rent their homes.
- Most people live in houses, but large numbers of flats are being built. Homes have improved, but more than a quarter are not properly maintained or constructed.
- House prices have been booming for more than a decade - almost tripling since 1996. The sharp increase has far outpaced wage rises.
- The average house now costs more than six times the average wage. In London the figure is closer to nine times.
- It has led to fears that many people will not be able to buy a first home, or a larger one.

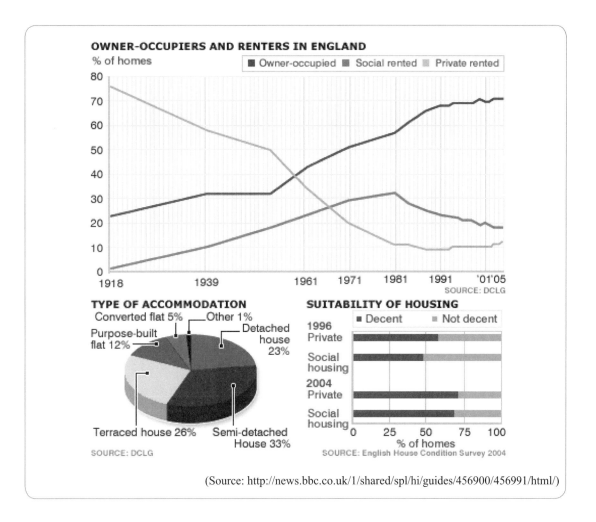

OWNER-OCCUPIERS AND RENTERS IN ENGLAND

% of homes

Legend: ■ Owner-occupied ■ Social rented ■ Private rented

SOURCE: DCLG

TYPE OF ACCOMMODATION

- Converted flat 5%
- Other 1%
- Purpose-built flat 12%
- Detached house 23%
- Terraced house 26%
- Semi-detached House 33%

SOURCE: DCLG

SUITABILITY OF HOUSING

Legend: ■ Decent ■ Not decent

1996 Private
Social housing
2004 Private
Social housing

% of homes

SOURCE: English House Condition Survey 2004

(Source: http://news.bbc.co.uk/1/shared/spl/hi/guides/456900/456991/html/)

- The typical first time buyer is now 33-years-old and takes five years to save the average £24,000 deposit (rising to £44,000 in London).
- It is thought that four out of 10 people buying a first home now rely on parental help.
- At 69%, the level of home ownership is high, but lower than Spain's 82%. Further afield, the rate is 84% in Slovenia and 94% in Hungary.
- Despite being one of Europe's most crowded nations, only one in 50 UK homes is in a block of four storeys or more.

FACTS & STATISICS – USA

- Residents of all EU nations have less space than those of the US, where a typical home is 163m/2.
- Government subsidized housing is called 'public housing' (aka 'the projects') and is intended for those on low salaries.
- These properties are usually in big apartment complexes, built for this purpose.
- Around 1 and a quarter million people live in public housing. In the past people from all backgrounds lived in public housing, but as ore families choose to buy a place to live modern day tenants are often very poor and/or suffering from various social problems e.g, poor health, unemployment, criminal activity, drug use.
- In recent times there has been a shift towards helping people with rent in the private sector, to beat the negative issues public housing can lead to.

U.S. Households- Renters & Owners

Type of Household	Households	% of U.S. Total	Residents	% of U.S. Total
Renter-Occupied	43,267,432	37%	110,175,847	35%
Owner-Occupied	73,991,995	63%	200,617,048	65%
Total	117,259,427	100%	310,792,895	100%

Source: NMHC tabulations of 2014 American Community Survey microdata. Updated 9/2015.

Note: Does not include non-housing units.

Tenure by Age of Population

Age Distribution	People in Rental Housing	Share	People in Owner-Occupied Housing	Share
Under 30 Years Old	55,216,242	51%	67,195,176	34%
30 to 44 Years Old	24,716,015	23%	36,042,790	18%
45 to 64 Years Old	19,562,510	18%	62,207,298	31%
65 Years and Older	8,079,103	8%	35,080,135	17%
Total	107,573,870	100%	200,525,299	100%

Source: NMHC tabulations of 2013 American Community Survey microdata. Updated 2/2014.

Note: Does not include non-housing units.

(Source: http://nmhc.org/Content.aspx?id=4708)

- In the USA around 6.5% of the population live in trailer parks. Many of them live in high quality homes, like the one in the picture, but others are poor, and their trailers are rundown, and on sites with lots of garbage and old cars around etc.

They are often called 'trailer trash', and live with the stigma of being on a low income and unable to buy or rent a regular property.

READING 1

The 10 Home Styles that are Most Popular Around America

Before you read

Look quickly at all the photographs of houses. Which one is your favorite? (One you would like to live in). Why? What appeals to you? Now take a closer look at each photo - don't read the words yet - can you identify any differences between the houses? You can make notes on any differences in the space below.

Vocabulary exercise

Look at the words below – check any you feel you don't know the meaning of, but don't use a dictionary yet to look for the meaning.

1. mass-produced	11. built-ins
2. fashionable	12. dining booths
3. original	13. wrap-around porches
4. master craftsman	14. operable shutters
5. bungalow	15. monumental columns.
6. 18th century colonists	16. Mediterranean
7. historically accurate	17. verandas
8. marble	18. interior
9. ranches	
10. sprawling	

In the reading you will see these words again, bolded. Try to work out the meaning of any you don't know through context – looking at the sentence the word is used in for clues. Don't stop to use a dictionary.

The 10 Home Styles that are Most Popular Around America

There are many different styles of houses available in America, and you will find different types are more popular in different parts of the country. Here, Marika Snider, of Snider Architecture, explains the different styles.

1. Craftsman style

Inspired by 'arts and crafts movement' homes first built in Europe around 1880 - 1910. At that time **mass-produced** things were very **fashionable**, which made some people want something **original**, made by a **master craftsman** and not a factory worker. The exteriors are usually made of stone and wood, and these homes are usually **bungalow** style.

2. Country style

A modern version of the 'Colonial style' home, which were influenced by **18th century colonists** bringing European styles with them. They're often have two windows on either side of the front door and five windows on top, with the middle window directly above the door. Country houses aspire to be warm and inviting, and often have wide porches and **shutters**.

3. Traditional style

A Traditional style house is similar to Country style but is more **historically accurate**.

4. European style

European style homes are based on house styles traditional to France, Italy and sometimes England. There's an emphasis on elements which look old but are durable, such as **marble** or high-quality stone floors, and massive fireplaces.

5. Ranch style

Originally used as housing on **ranches**, the term has come to mean any story house. Because the entire house is on one floor, Ranch houses can be **sprawling**. This style was very popular in the 1950s and '60s.

6. Farmhouse

Farmhouses are usually a rectangle shape and often have some 19th century design influences, such as tall, narrow windows and large porches.

7. Cottage style

Cottages are smaller houses or bungalows with details inspired by the 1920s, when a typical cottage would have a generous front porch, with a second story typically tucked into the **attic**. The interior might include **built-ins** like window seats, display cases or **dining booths**.

8. Modern style

Popular in the 1950s and '60s, modern houses have flat or lower slope roofs, horizontal windows and large, undecorated fireplaces. They don't have lots of details - plain lines are important.

9. Southern style

In the southern part of America the weather is often very hot and humid, so this house style is designed to keep people inside as cool as possible. You will see elevated main living levels, **wraparound porches**, and large **operable shutters**. Southern style homes might also have 19th century details like **monumental columns** at the entrance.

10. Mediterranean style

Mediterranean style houses are inspired by homes in southern Spain, France, and Italy. They typically focus on patios, courtyards and **verandas** as ways to extend the house outdoors. The outside of these homes usually have few details, and the **interior** detailing is simple.

CREDIT 클리핑 위치: http://www.huffingtonpost.com/2015/01/15/popular-home-styles_n_6460034.html>
Monday, October 5, 2015

MORE READING/INFO
https://en.wikipedia.org/wiki/Arts_and_Crafts_movement

READING 2

Ana Finds an Apartment

Read the story. Then answer the questions below.

Ana, her husband Mario, and their four-year-old son, Antonio, just moved to North Carolina. They need a temporary place to live until they can save enough to buy their own home. Right now, they are staying in a hotel not far from Mario's job.

Ana begins a search for an apartment for the family to live in. First, she picks up an Apartment Book at the local newspaper stand. This special book contains listings of all the major apartment complexes in her area.

Ana starts by looking at the prices for apartments, then she reads about the amenities that each apartment complex offers. For example, some apartments have a clubhouse, some have a gym - which is also called a fitness center - some have a pool. Some have all of these! Ana notices that the more amenities an apartment complex has, the more it costs each month.

She wants the family's new apartment to be nice, but she doesn't want to spend too much money on it. After considering prices, amenities, and locations, Ana finds several apartment complexes that she thinks the family will like.

Ana calls five apartment managers and makes plans to see their places. When Mario gets back to the hotel from work, Ana shows him the list of apartments. "These look good," he says. The next day, while Mario is at work and Antonio is at daycare, Ana visits the apartment complexes.

She likes the fifth one the best. It is in a good school district. It has a pool, but no fitness center or clubhouse. It is near Mario's job. Ana hopes to find a job nearby as well. When Ana gets back to the hotel, she discusses all that she has seen with Mario. They decide to rent the last apartment Ana saw.

The next day, Ana calls the manager of the apartment complex with the news. The manager asks Ana and Mario to sign a lease and pay a security deposit. If the family damages the apartment in any way the security deposit will help to pay for the cost of repairs.

Ana and Mario sign a lease, pay the money, and make plans to move in a few days. Finally, they have a place to stay.

(Adapted from http://www.englishforeveryone.org/PDFs/Ana_Finds_An_Apartment.pdf)

Comprehension Questions for Reading 2

1) What kind of book does Ana get?
   A. A City Guide Book
   B. A Map Book
   C. A House Book
   D. An Apartment Book

2) What did Ana consider while looking through the Apartment Book?
   A. school districts
   B. amenities.
   C. locations
   D. school districts & amenities
   E. amenities & locations
   F. all three things

3) Where is Ana's family staying while they look for a place to call home?
   A. in an apartment close to Mario's work
   B. at an apartment next to Antonio's school
   C. in Ana's mother's house
   D. in a hotel near Mario's work

4) What does Ana realize as she looks through the Apartment Book?
   A. that the nicest apartments are far away
   B. that all the apartments are small and cramped
   C. that it is easy to find a nice apartment in a good school district
   D. that the number of amenities is related to cost

5) Why doesn't Ana want to spend too much money on an apartment?
   A. Her husband will get upset.
   B. She does not have the money.
   C. She cannot find one she likes.
   D. She wants to save money for a house.

6) As described in the beginning of the story, which of the following is not mentioned as an amenity?
   A. carpet
   B. clubhouse
   C. fitness center
   D. pool

7) What makes Ana like the fifth apartment best?

    A. It has many amenities.

    B. It is in a good school district

    C. It has a parking lot.

8) Where is Antonio while Ana looks at apartments?

    A. at daycare

    B. at the hotel

    C. at school

    D. at work

9) As described in the middle of the story, what does it mean to consider something?

    A. to rent it

    B. to think about it

    C. to make it happen

    D. to read a book about it

10) "When Ana gets back to the hotel, she discusses all that she has seen with Mario." Which of the following is the best way to rewrite the above sentence while keeping its meaning the same?

    A.When Ana gets back to the hotel, she reads about all she has seen with Mario.

    B. When Ana returns to the hotel, she writes about all she has seen with Mario.

    C. When Ana returns to the hotel, she talks about all she has seen with Mario.

    D. When Ana leaves the hotel, she talks about all she has seen with Mario.

11) When will the family move into their new apartment?

    A. the next day

    B. at the first of the month

    C. in three or four days

    D. in just over a week

12) As used at the end of the story, which is the best description of a security deposit?

    A. money given to landlord to pay for amenities

    B. money given to landlord to pay for utilities and telephone

    C. money given to landlord to prove the tenant can pay rent on time

    D. money given to the landlord to pay for any damage to the apartment

Jigsaw Activity for Reading 2

(Follow the instructions your teacher gives you very closely. Teacher instructions are given in the Answer Section)

Rebecca's On The Move

(A)

Rebecca Briggs is 22 years old and she just started working in her first job after graduating from university. She's got a great job but it is 100 miles from her family home – too far to travel every day. She has to find a new place to live – in a new town, and that is going to be expensive.

(B)

After a week of looking at rental apartments Rebecca knows she can't find anything nice with her small budget for housing. She doesn't know what to do until a friend suggests looking online for house-share ads. Rebecca finds lots of websites run these ads – and there are plenty of places she can afford to look at, but she isn't sure living with strangers will be fun.

(C)

It's one month later and Rebecca has moved into a house-share. She has a large, private bedroom in a big house. She shares the bathroom with one other girl, and the kitchen and lounge with everyone. There are four people in the house and they are all friendly and nice.

FOOD 6

INTRODUCTION

Before you start

- What's your favorite food?
- How often do you eat it?
- What kinds of food are popular in your country?
- What's unpopular?

Look at Maslow's pyramid of human needs (**Chapter 1**). How important is food in his opinion?

Food is essential to life, and a major part of most cultures around the world. Relationships between people and food may be about survival, pleasure, power, status, guilt, fun, good health – or bad.

Within one country there will be people who are struggling to eat enough, along with those who are struggling to lose weight after eating too much.

Food can tell you lots of things about culture. By studying -

- what people eat
- when and how often they eat
- where they buy the ingredients/food
- how their food is prepared and served

- you can get lots of clues which tell you about a person's:

- location - some foods are cheap, readily available and/or produced domestically/personally
- ethnicity - identified by high consumption levels of certain dishes or ingredients
- socio-economic class – higher classes have more variety in their diet and often eat less pre-prepared food
- religion and moral values - animals may be killed/cooked in a certain way, some foods/killing methods are taboo

Be critical of what you read and see in this class. That means don't just accept things are the same for everyone.

FACTS

- Potatoes, rice or bread are popular staples in the UK and the USA.
- In the UK and USA people like to eat different staple food at each meal. Say cereal for breakfast, bread at lunchtime and potatoes in the evening.
- In the USA 'family restaurants' like Denny's and Olive Garden are very popular, but in the UK this role is filled more by pubs. Many people go to traditional restaurants for special events such as dates, celebrations or similar.
- Americans eat enough hamburgers every year to circle the earth 32 times!
- The five most popular foods in the USA are: steak, chicken, pizza, waffles and beef. (The first fruit to make the list is the blueberry, at #18).
- The five most popular foods in the UK are: chicken tikka masala, spaghetti bolognese, a roast dinner, chilli con carne and cottage or shepherd's pie.

Confusing terms

Sometimes native English speakers misunderstand the meaning of a word. This is especially common with the names we used for meals.

Meal name	UK/US - Lower social classes	UK/US – Higher social classes
Breakfast	Generally means the same to everyone. First meal of the day.	Generally means the same to everyone. First meal of the day.
Midday meal	Often called dinner	Generally called lunch
Evening meal	Often called tea (a full cooked meal with 1-2 courses)	Mostly called dinner or supper (a full cooked meal with 2-3 courses)
Food after evening meal	Called supper (light food, perhaps crackers and cheese or some cookies, a yogurt etc).	————

Although social class influences the terms we use for meals there is also a regional difference.

'Dinner' usually refers to the biggest meal of the day. In agricultural or manual work fields this would usually be eaten at lunchtime, while richer or higher class people ate their heaviest meal in the evening.

Vocabulary on UK and USA Foods

In the USA you go to the store or market to buy your produce. You use a cart to collect your items, stand in line to pay at the checkout, where someone will ask if you need help to bag your food.

In the UK you go to the supermarket to buy your fruit and veg. You use a trolley to collect your items, then queue to pay at the till, where someone will ask you if you need help to pack your bags.

British and American Food Words
Write the number of the correct match next to each word

( ) Aubergine	1 - Pop/Soda/Coke
( ) Courgette	2 - Cookie
( ) Biscuit	3 - Popsicle
( ) Chips	4 - Fries
( ) Chocolate bar	5 - Zucchini
( ) Crisps	6 - Candy
( ) Fizzy drink	7 - Oatmeal
( ) Ice lolly	8 - Potato chips
( ) Porridge	9 - Eggplant
( ) Sweets	10 - Candy bar

STATISTICS

- The average UK family spends 11% of their income on food. (2014)
- The average UK household throws away around £470 (725 US$) worth of eatable food each year. (2014)
- 1 in 100 UK residents suffer from an intolerance to gluten. (meaning they cannot eat regular bread, pasta etc)
- Between 7 – 11% of UK residents are vegetarian, 1% are vegan.
- Over 4.7 million people in the UK live in food poverty (not enough to eat), The exact figure is hard to find because many people don't ask for help.
- In the USA (2014) 14% of the population were either partly or seriously 'food insecure' (not always having access to food).
- 1 in 4 Americans eat some kind of fast food every day.
- In one year the average American eats around 280kg of dairy products but only 124kg of fruit.

THEORY

There are various ways to explain the role of food in society from a theoretical viewpoint. Here is a very brief overview of some key points.

CLASS

Left wing theorists may say that poor/lower class people don't have the same access to food as others. They may spend their lives in a cycle of trying to find enough food to stay alive, leaving them no time or energy to get organized into a group and complain enough to change the situation. Because processed food is generally either cheaper or more filling $ for $/£ for £ the poor eat an unhealthy diet. The richer people don't care about this when the economy is weak, but if the poor were needed for work or to fight a war, (to make society function well) then they would be given enough food to get healthier.

Right wing thinkers would say we have a personal or individual responsibility to provide food for our family, and that helping poor people out will not help them change and find work/money.

Feminist thinkers claim that food ties women to the domestic realm, and that being responsible for food collection, preparation and production – even if she has a paid job too – controls her life and time.

How accurate are these ideas?

It is true that during the second war (1935-1945) a special food stem called 'rationing' was introduced. During WW1 many British people had died due to an inadequate diet so the government wanted to share out available food more equally during WW2. Many poor people ate better than before the war and women were able to keep the country's farms and factories in operation.

In modern times both the USA and the UK have large groups of people who are not short of food to eat, but they are lacking the healthy food their body needs to work properly. They have unbalanced diets.

These people are often called the 'working poor', because they have work but it is low paid, and they do not have enough money spare to either eat enough, or to eat well. They may of course understand which foods are healthier, but they cannot think beyond survival.

It is possible to buy healthy foods for lower prices in large supermarkets – but the problem is many of these are now located out of the main towns. Without a car it is difficult to use them. Buying from small, local shops usually adds about 10% to the costs of food items.

Poorer people are much more likely to develop a serious illness or health condition as a result of their poor diet.

Of course people with more money also eat unhealthy foods, and suffer from being overweight and related health problems. But these are much more common in poorer families and communities.

Basically, the more money you have and the higher your social class, the more likely you are to make food choices based on:

- Food quality (rather than price)
- Where it was produced (local is best, reduced carbon footprint/food miles)
- Organic certification?
- Fairtrade?
- The producer getting a fair price
- Independent store bought rather than supermarket chain
- Fresh over processed
- Variety of food in diet

Overall it does appear that the key factor in our relationship with food in UK and US culture is social class. The higher up the scale you are the more food is about pleasure, nutrition, fun, entertainment, choice and the environment. While for the poorest it is simply about survival.

READING

Work with another student. One of you will read this page, the other version B on page 86. You need to ask your partner questions to fill in the spaces.

Reading 1 (Version A) - What is British Food?

Many foreigners think of British food as being things like fish and chips. They may also use words like (1) _____, _____ and _____ when describing the way British food tastes.

Is this fair? Or are these ideas based on stereotypes which are passed on without any direct experience of the range of British dishes?

It is probably fair to say that British food doesn't depend on spices the way Indian or Korean food often does, but there are plenty of spicy (hot) dishes on the average UK households menu, and lots of food which is cooked with herbs for added flavour.

British cuisine has always been influenced by other cultures, which means it has adapted through history to accommodate new ingredients and styles of cooking.

Who brought the UK which foods?

- The Romans (55 BC) – apples, pears, grapes carrots
- The _____ (793 AD) - taught Brits to smoke fish
- 16th century – explorers discovered new lands and brought back: sugar (The Caribbean), cocoa and coffee (South America); potatoes (America).
- Victorian period (1837 – 1901) –British food was transformed with exotic spices from the countries Britain ruled at that time.

During both great wars (1914-1919 and 1939-1945) food was in short supply, so most people had to make do with boring, plain meals.

Traditional British dishes (similar perhaps to the wartime diet) are still popular.

These include:
- Shepherd's Pie - (minced lamb and vegetables in gravy in a dish, covered with mashed potato).
- Pastry based pies, with either meat or fruit filling.
- Sausage (_____) and Mash – sausages served with mashed potatoes

- Bread & Butter Pudding – bread slices with butter on them, soaked in milk and cooked in the oven with dried fruit.

After WW2 many immigrants came to Britain to help fill the vacant jobs. And many of these were from the former Colonies. They changed the face of British food again, as did other immigrants who came over in later years.

In most British towns and cities these days you will find restaurants and takeaways offering Chinese, Indian, Greek, Italian, Mexican and Middle-Eastern food. Larger cities will have food from every corner of the world available. Many recipes have been adapted over the years to suit British tastes.

Roast beef (or pork, lamb, chicken) is still a very food to serve on a Sunday. Usually this is a family meal, eaten at _____, and including:

Roast meat
Yorkshire puddings
Roast and mashed potatoes
Several vegetables
Gravy
Sauces to match the meat

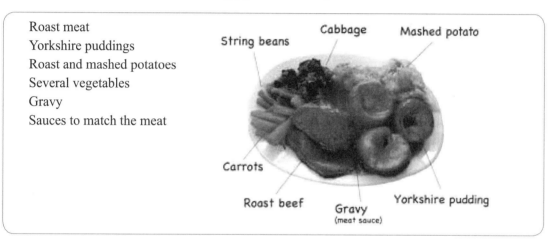

These days British people like to source food from all around the world, eating lamb from New Zealand, exotic fruit like mangoes, and some are happy to pay more for organic produce.

Fish and seafood are always important to an island county, although in the UK they are quite expensive. Prawns, cod, pollack, haddock and tuna are all popular. You may be surprised to her though that the average UK resident eats fish and chips only 5-6 times a year.

Questions to ask your partner (who is reading version B)

1. How would foreigners maybe describe British food?
2. Who taught British people to smoke fish?
3. What is the slang word for sausages?
4. What time do most people eat a Sunday roast?

Reading 1 (Version B) - What is British Food?

Many foreigners think of British food as being things like _____. They may also use words like heavy, greasy and bland when describing the way British food tastes.

Is this fair? Or are these ideas based on stereotypes which are passed on without any direct experience of the range of British dishes?

It is probably fair to say that British food doesn't depend on spices the way Indian or Korean food often does, but there are plenty of spicy (hot) dishes on the average UK households menu, and lots of food which is cooked with herbs for added flavour.

British cuisine has always been influenced by other cultures, which means it has adapted through history to accommodate new ingredients and styles of cooking.

Who brought the UK which foods?

- The Romans (55 BC) – apples, pears, grapes carrots
- The Vikings (793 AD) - taught Brits to smoke fish
- 16th century – explorers discovered new lands and brought back: sugar (The Caribbean), cocoa and coffee (South America); potatoes (America).
- Victorian period (1837 – 1901) –British food was transformed with exotic spices from the countries Britain ruled at that time.

During both great wars (1914-1919 and 1939-1945) food was in short supply, so most people had to make do with boring, plain meals.

Traditional British dishes (similar perhaps to the wartime diet) are still popular.

These include:
- Shepherd's Pie - (minced lamb and vegetables in gravy in a dish, covered with _____).
- Pastry based pies, with either meat or fruit filling.
- Sausage (bangers) and Mash – sausages served with mashed potatoes
- Bread & Butter Pudding – bread slices with butter on them, soaked in milk and cooked in the oven with dried fruit.

After WW2 many immigrants came to Britain to help fill the vacant jobs. And many of these were from the former Colonies. They changed the face of British food again, as did other immigrants who came over in later years.

In most British towns and cities these days you will find restaurants and takeaways offering

Chinese, Indian, Greek, Italian, Mexican and Middle-Eastern food. Larger cities will have food from every corner of the world available. Many recipes have been adapted over the years to suit British tastes.

Roast beef (or pork, lamb, chicken) is still a very food to serve on a Sunday. Usually this is a family meal, eaten at lunchtime, and including:

Roast meat
Yorkshire puddings
Roast and mashed potatoes
Several vegetables
Gravy
Sauces to match the meat

String beans   Cabbage   Mashed potato

Carrots

Roast beef   Gravy
(meat sauce)   Yorkshire pudding

These days British people like to source food from all around the world, eating lamb from New Zealand, exotic fruit like mangoes, and some are happy to pay more for organic produce.

Fish and seafood are always important to an island county, although in the UK they are quite expensive. Prawns, cod, pollack, haddock and tuna are all popular. You may be surprised to her though that the average UK resident eats fish and chips only _____ times a year.

Questions to ask your partner (who is reading version A)

1. Which food do foreigners usually associate with Britain?
2. What is shepherds pie covered with?
3. What day do families often get together to eat a joint of meat on?
4. How often does the average British person eat fish and chips?

READING 2

What a British Person Should Know When Eating Out in America

Eating out may be a simple thing, but for British people who have just come to America it could be an experience full of surprises. Here are five main differences a Brit should pay attention to when eating out in a restaurant in America.

Ordering Drinks

The first thing a waiter will ask when you sit down in an American restaurant is whether you would like bottled or tap water. If you choose bottled, you will then be asked whether you would prefer still or sparkling.

Soon, the water you ordered will be brought to you. Coffee and soft drinks will also be gladly refilled. The waiter will ask you often if you want another coffee or coke. In Britain, water and soft drinks must be requested and they are not free.

The Service

Waiters in American restaurants are more pleasant and attentive. They are always chatty and often come to your table during the meal to refill drinks and check everything is okay.

In England, waiters are less likely to frequently check on customers. If you need something, you can raise your hand and wave at the waiter but otherwise you will be left alone for hours.

The Menu

In an American restaurant, picky eaters can customize the menu to suit their exact preferences by reeling off special requirements and substitutions. You can order salad but without tomato, or with a special dressing to accommodate your diet. There is a friendly atmosphere that encourages you to have exactly what you want and satisfy your appetite.

On the other hand, people in England tend to order a meal with all the options that come with it. It is less common for them to complain about the food or have the waiter send dishes back to the kitchen.

Picking up the Bill

In America, a waiter will bring you the bill even though you have not asked for it. This would be seen as very impolite by British customers, as it implies that they are being hurried out of the restaurant. British people either ask the waiter to bring the bill or they go to the cashier and pay.

Tipping

Tipping in England is optional. You will tip if you are satisfied with the meal and service, which is generally about 10%. If you are not happy with the service or the food you do not need to tip, and many people choose to take this option.

In America, a tip of 15-20% is generally mandatory. For American waiters, tipping is the main source of their income. Even if the service is bad you should still tip, but it makes sense to give a smaller tip.

(Author's note – I am British and have been to America several times too, and I don't agree with everything that this article says. If you go to a good restaurant it is normal to be offered a drink as soon as you are seated, and you wouldn't generally be charged for drinking tap water. As for tips, it is pretty standard to tip after a meal in a restaurant, but not so much in a café. Valerie)

Comprehension questions for Reading 2

1) What would a waiter ask first in an American restaurant?
   a) Whether you would like water or a soft drink.
   b) Whether you would like bottled or tap water.
   c) Whether you would like coffee.
   d) Whether you would like a cocktail.

2) What is a waiter in Britain less likely to do than an American waiter?
   a) Check on customers.
   b) Ask for tips.
   c) Bring the menu.
   d) Take an order.

3) What are British customers likely to do when eating out?
   a) Ask for something on the menu to be cooked differently.
   b) Complain to the waiter about food that they don't like.
   c) Order everything on the menu.
   d) Order a meal, even if they don't want something that is included with it.

4) How do customers pick up the bill in British restaurants?
   a) Wait until a waiter brings it.
   b) Put money on the table.
   c) Ask the waiter for it.
   d) Go to the cashier.

5) How much should you tip a waiter in America?
   a) Less than $10.
   b) About 10%.
   c) Between $15 and $20.
   d) Between 15 and 20%.

(Adapted from http://www.excellentesl4u.com/esl-eating-out-reading.html)

EDUCATION 7

INTRODUCTION

Before you read

- Think about the education system in your country.
- Can you speak English well? Is this due to school education?
- How does education influence a country?

Most cultures in the world have some form of education system in place, but what 'educating' actually means, and how it is delivered in practice, tends to vary between cultures.

In the USA and the UK education takes a quite traditional form – young people spend a lot of their life in a building (school), studying, taking tests and trying to get paper qualifications.

Many other countries in the world also have a traditional approach to education, however, in the US and the UK what happens in the classroom, the subjects studied and the way lessons are delivered may be very different from say schools in Asia. You'll learn more about this later.

A key question considered in this unit is: what is education for? (What role does it play in society?) This topic is examined in the theory section.

There is also lots of extra information about everything from timetables to uniforms and school food.

FACTS

About Education in the USA

- The right to education for all - including the disabled and the disadvantaged.
- Mandatory to attend school, though children can be educated at home.
- Student-centered education
- Problem based learning
- Focus on creativity
- State Department of Education & State Board of Education
- 12 years of education (K-12)
- Mostly funded/controlled by the government, at national (federal), state (region) and local levels
- School year begins in August
- Educational Mission: ED's mission is to promote student achievement and preparation for global competitiveness by fostering educational excellence and ensuring equal access.
- Around 10% of American children attend private (fee paying) schools)
- Approx ¼ of children in regular education are performing under the expected grade level for their age
- Around 85% of adult Americans have completed high school
- Around a quarter of the US adult population have an undergraduate, or higher, degree.

(Partly from: http://www2.ed.gov/about/overview/mission/mission.html)

[Key phrases you may wish to research: Class of 2013; No Child Left Behind Act of 2001; Recruit, Prepare, Retain, and Reward America's Teachers (Obama)]

About Education in the UK

- Education is free at all stages.
- All children must attend full time school (or equivalent) from age 4/5 – 16/18.*
- There are two stages to the compulsory UK education:
    primary (4/5 - 11)
    secondary (11 – 16/18*)
- Teachers are generally referred to by title and surname. e.g. Miss Brown
- All state funded schools must follow the National Curriculum. (Private schools can avoid

this.)

- The school year runs from September – June and is 39 weeks long.
- School holidays total around 13 weeks. 6 weeks in the summer, 2 each at Easter and Christmas, and 2 x one week breaks at the end of October and mid-February.
- From 14 - 16 students study for examinations called GCSEs. Part of their final grade comes from coursework done throughout this time, and part from a final test.
- Most schools start between 8.30 - 9 am and finish between 3.30 – 4 pm, with an hour for lunch and two breaks, mid morning and afternoon.
- In state schools maths, English a science, religious instruction and physical education, along with a computing related subject are compulsory for 14-16 year olds.
- Students are generally free to choose the other subjects they would like to study. These may be called electives, or options, and they are also 2 year long courses with tests and assessments.

(*This depends on where you live in the UK, see
https://www.gov.uk/know-when-you-can-leave-school for full details)

Public Schools in the UK

Headington School, Oxford, UK

Many foreigners may be confused by the term 'public schools'. What makes things difficult for them to understand is the fact that these schools are nor 'public' at all. If fact, they are private schools. In order to explain the existence of this large group of private schools outside the state system, and the seeming paradox of their name, one has to go into their history.

Some of the oldest public schools in Britain are very old indeed and when they were originally founded, or endowed, they were intended by their founders to provide education for the sons of parents who were too poor to educate them privately. Such schools did provide a kind of public education and the name 'public' school remained although their character, over the years radically changed.

One of the reasons for the growth of the 'public schools' in the nineteenth century was the absence of a good state school system. Today, in spite of the increasing high fees, which have to be paid, the 'public school' is more sought after than ever before.

(Reading Source: M.D. Munro Mackenzie & L.J. Westwood, *Background to Britain*)

STATISTICS

Can you read the graphs below to understand the college enrollment rates?

US education statistics

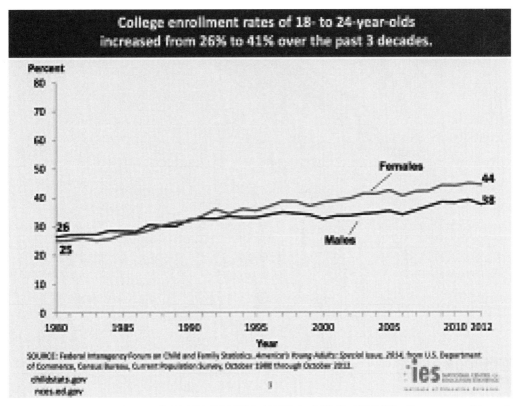

(http://www.usnews.com/cmsmedia/c3/48/a60300784ed186026aa05f858cdf/140922collegewm-graphic.png)

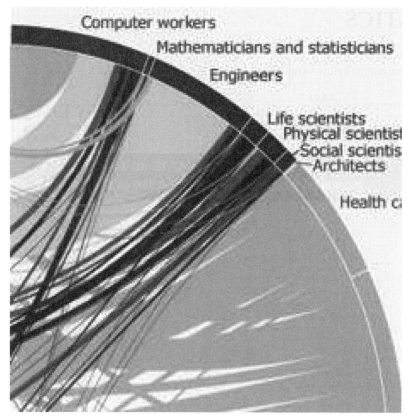

(See full image at http://www.census.gov/dataviz/visualizations/stem/stem-html/)

UK education statistics

- Around 94% of children attend free, state funded schools, and around 6% attend 'private' (fee-paying) schools.
- The exact numbers of children being 'home schooled' is unknown, but it is thought to be less than 0.5%.
- Most students study for 5 – 12 GCSE's
- Just under 50% of the UK population attend university. Education is free, and compulsory for all children between the ages of 5 - 16.
- Children's education in England is normally divided into two separate stages. They begin with primary education at the age of five and this usually lasts until they are eleven. Then they move to secondary school, there they stay until they reach sixteen, seventeen or eighteen years of age.
- Teachers are always addressed by their surname by parents and pupils alike, always Mr, Mrs or Miss Smith.
- All government-run schools, state schools, follow the same National Curriculum.
- The school year runs from September to July and is 39 weeks long.
- The main school holidays are: Christmas- 2 weeks, spring - 2 weeks, summer - 6 weeks. There are also one week holidays in October, February and May.
- Children normally start primary school at the age of four or five, but many schools now have a reception year for four year olds. Children normally leave at the age of 11, moving on to secondary school.
- At the age of 16, students in England, Wales and Northern Ireland take an examination called the GCSE (General Certificate of Secondary Education). Study of GSCE subjects begins at the start of Year 10 (age 14-15), and final examinations are then taken at the end of Year 11 (age 15-16).
- In state schools English, Mathematics, Science, Religious Education and Physical Education are studied during Key Stage 4 (the GCSE years of school); in England, some form of ICT and citizenship must be studied and, in Wales, Welsh must be studied. Other subjects, chosen by the individual pupil, are also studied.
- After completing the GCSE, some students leave school, others go onto technical college, whilst others continue at high school for two more years and take a further set of standardized exams, known as A levels, in three or four subjects. These exams determine whether a student is eligible for university.

Task: Can you identify the things the UK and US education system have in common, and the differences?

THEORY

Explanations of why the education system exists

There are several different theories which hold quite different views on the reason for/role of education in society.

Remember the key point - that most cultures have some form of education in place, even if the way this is delivered is not uniform. However, the underlying role of education is generally always to 'teach people what they need to know.'

Where people differ is on who decides what people need to know, and why.

Here are some of the main viewpoints:

- Education is a way to control young people, and keep them out of trouble. If they are busy all day they cannot get together and challenge the system. (which is what young people tend to want to do)
- Education systems in the UK and the US are set up to make sure only some people can achieve. The rich and the naturally bright have too many advantages and the poor and those who learn in different ways fall behind - which means they never have the same opportunities.
- Education in western countries is the key way people can be tested and sorted into suitable roles for their ability and intelligence. Not all can achieve the same, but all are important.

Harvard Old Yard, USA

School meals – UK

<Typical primary school menu for school lunch>

Monday	Tuesday	Wednesday	Thursday	Friday
Lamb & Apricot Curry Cannelloni with Spinach topped with Parmesan Cheese or Filled Jacket Potato	Beef Burger with Peppercorn Sauce or Chickpea and Napolitaine & Basil Penne	Roasted Chicken Legs or Jacket Potatoes filled with Lentils & Savoury Tomato Rice	Sweet & Sour Pork or Sneaky Pie Filled Jacket Potato	Fish Fingers or Broccoli & Macaroni with a Herby Crust
Boiled Rice Garden Peas	Cream & Chive Potatoes Broccoli	Roast Potatoes Braised Red Cabbage	Brown Rice Carrots & Swede	Chipped Potatoes Baked Beans
Mixed Salad	Mixed Salad	Mixed Salad	Mixed Salad	Mixed Salad
Hot Apple Turnovers & Cream or Pineapple & Kiwi Slices	Cornflake Tart or Raspberry Rice Pudding	Rhubarb Crunch & Caramel Custard or Yoghurt	Warm Bakewell Tart or Fresh Fruit Salad	Ginger Sponge Pudding or Cheese & Biscuits

In the UK children generally eat lunch in the school dining hall. In primary school you may sit at designated tables, but in secondary school and beyond you are free to choose.

Mostly students are free to choose the food they want to. Special staff cook and serve the food and wash the dishes later.

Q. How does this compare to school lunch in your country?

ELECTIVES (Free choice subjects)

It's standard practice for western school children to choose a lot of the classes they attend. These classes are known as 'electives' and may focus on traditional subjects, physical activity, language or skills development.

Place these elective (chosen) subjects into the correct categories.

French	Dance
School newspaper	Gymnastics
Radio broadcasting	Orchestra
Basketball	Carpentry
Web design	Creative writing
Woodworking	Drama
Spanish	Sculpture
Choir	Photography
Tennis	German

Performing arts	
Visual arts	
Vocational education	
Physical education	
Foreign languages	
Journalism/publishing	

Answer the questions:

1. Do you think offering student's some choice in subjects is a good idea in middle and high school? Why, or why not?

2. Did you have any opportunity to choose your own subjects?

3. Do you have any ideas for interesting elective classes?

RESEARCH

- What is MOOC?
- Visit www.edx.org / www.coursera.org
- How will Education change in the US and UK?
- Are there similar changes in your country?

INTRODUCTION

Before We Start

- How can we define leisure?
- Is it a term which describes what humans do for fun?
- Is any time not spent at work or on domestic duties leisure time?
- Is free time always leisure time?
- Is leisure time something that is experienced differently between people due to age, class, gender, nationality?

Read the following words carefully. Would you link them to your idea of what 'leisure' is? You can choose to answer YES , NO , or NOT SURE (but do try to make a definite choice)

going to the gym

housework/chores

gardening

DIY

shopping

watching a movie

walking your dog

eating in a restaurant

Now compare your ideas with some other people in your class, and discuss any different opinions you have.

Did you have the same opinions as your classmates? It's actually quite difficult to decide which activities can be classed as leisure and which not, partly because the way we define the term 'leisure' is not always uniform.

Is leisure describing:

- things we do in our free time
- things we do for fun
- things we do which are not connected to any kind of work

or is it something else?

All of the activities listed at the start could be classed as leisure, or as paid work, depending on context!!

In general the terms leisure and free time, (as in time not spent in a paid work environment), do not have the same meaning.

For example:

a one hour lunch break is free time, but it is unlikely you'd do anything considered leisure based in that time. People who have to do chores in the house and garden after work do so in their free time but not may would count those tasks as leisure activities.

Some people though do enjoy what others see as chores, so although I hate gardening, if you love it then it may well be a leisure time activity for you. The same thing applies to DIY, cooking or anything really.

Imagine a typical person's day.
The free time they have and how they spend it varies a lot.

	Student (-18)	Student@college	Stay at home parent	Works outside the home
7 a.m.	Wakes/eats	Wakes/eats	Wakes/makes food & eats/childcare/chores	Wakes/makes food & eats/childcare/chores
8 a.m.	Goes to school	Goes to college	Chores/childcare	Commutes to work (may drop child(ren) at daycare
9-12 a.m.	Studies	Studies	Chores/childcare	Work
12-1p.m.	Lunch	Lunch	Chores/ childcare	Lunch
1-3 p.m.	School/play time	School or go shopping	Chores/ childcare	Work
3-6 p.m.	Homework Eats dinner	Homework May have chores Computer games Eats dinner	Chores/makes dinner	Work, commute home, dinner
6-bedtime	Watches TV	Meet friends	Chores Gardening Maybe go to the gym or meet a friend	Chores Gardening Meet friend Shopping

How much free time or leisure time does each person have? Is it easy to work it out?

(Source: https://upload.wikimedia.org/wikipedia/commons/c/c6/Surfing_on_the_Gold_Coast.jpg)

You have to decide for yourself what really counts as leisure and leisure time.
Remember:

- some people say leisure time is any free time we have after we are finished with work, school, doing household related tasks, eating, sleeping, and so on, while others think
- many people find pleasure in tasks others see as non-leisure related, or that we may feel pressure to do certain tasks in our free time to maintain face, e.g. the gardening.

(Source: https://upload.wikimedia.org/wikipedia/commons/1/1f
/Lion_dance_at_Wikimania_2013_opening_ceremory_7.jpg)

FACTS

US Sport

- Watching or taking part in sport is a part of everyday life in the USA.

- US citizens spend a lot of money on sports and things connected to them, like clothing.

- There are popular sporting activities for all ages, genders and classes.

- Many sports, recreation and athletic events and activities are supported financially by public money or private sponsorship.

- Native Americans played a different (earlier version) of both hockey and lacrosse.

- Sports competitions and activities became really popular from the late 19th century - around 1880s and on. Until then the church controlled sports and often banned them due to concern about 'physical pleasure' (your body should never make you feel good).

- Also at this time paid work was becoming less physical, so people needed to find another way to get exercise. Later people started to move into towns and drive cars, so again exercise was important.

- Organized sports are seen as great ways to focus emotion, burn off negative feelings and create community and national bonds.

- (American) football started after the 1850s and grew to become the major part of life it is today.

- Basketball and ice hockey are popular too.

- Interest in sports grew again when TVs became a part of most households.

- These days, individual sporting activities such as running jogging, biking or hang gliding are popular too, with many people choosing to exercise for fitness and not just for fun.

- in the 20th century more women and people from ethnic minorities have participated in US sport, even though both were excluded, by law, for many years from playing against or with men/white teams

- These days US sport represents freedom and equality, something anyone can get involved with no matter their age, class, ethnicity or gender. (At least in theory!)

Activity 1 - Introduction to UK Leisure

Match the picture with a category.

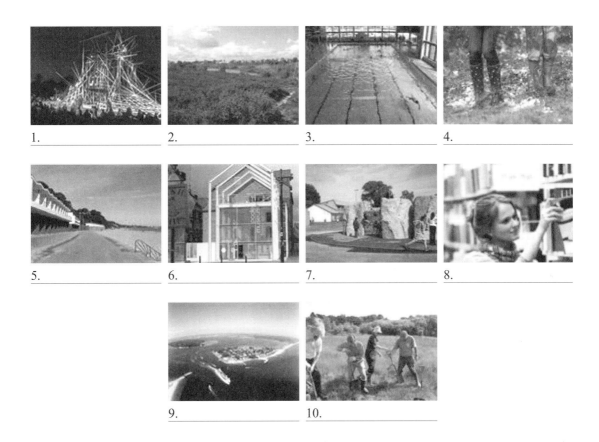

1. _____

2. _____

3. _____

4. _____

5. _____

6. _____

7. _____

8. _____

9. _____

10. _____

---

1. beaches
2. museums and local history
3. libraries
4. arts & entertainment
5. tourism and travel

6. leisure projects
7. events
8. parks and open spaces
9. sports clubs and fitness
10. volunteering

(Adapted from http://www.poole.gov.uk/leisure-and-culture/)

Activity 2 -British sports and leisure

Most of Britain's population enjoys sport and leisure activities in one way or another, and whether as a participant or a spectator there are a whole host of activities to enjoy.

Before you watch: Vocabulary

Match the words and phrases in the table to their definitions.

1. leisure ( )	2. participant ( )	3. spectator ( )	4. a whole host of ( )	5. whatever happens ( )
6.encouragement ( )	7. fit ( )	8. indoors ( )	9. recreation centres ( )	10.sedate ( )

Definitions:

a. words that make something more likely to happen
b. person involved in an activity
c. in any event
d. time when you are not working
e. person who only watches an activity or event
f. calm and relaxed
g. healthy and strong
h. inside a building
i. a large number of
j. public buildings for sports and activities

Task

Now watch the video and check if you got them right.

(Source: British Council VIDEO https://learnenglish.britishcouncil.org/en/uk-culture/leisure)

Comprehension Task

Reorder the words and phrases to make correct sentences about leisure in the UK. Write the sentences below.

1	in the UK	Most people	either actively	are involved	in recreational pursuits.	_____
2	in keep fit	are engaging	activities	More people	than in the past.	_____
3	sport inside	pay to join	You can do	for free or	or outside	a sports club.
4	time activities	Many free	in nature.	are	less strenuous	_____
5	Most urban areas	irrespective of	age.	will have something	to suit you,	_____

1. _____ .

2. _____ .

3. _____ .

4. _____ .

5. _____ .

Discussion

Q. What are the three most popular leisure activities in your country?
   How fit is your generation compared to previous ones?

(Source https://learnenglish.britishcouncil.org/en/uk-culture/leisure)

READING 1

The Land of Leisure

Why Americans have plenty of time to read this.

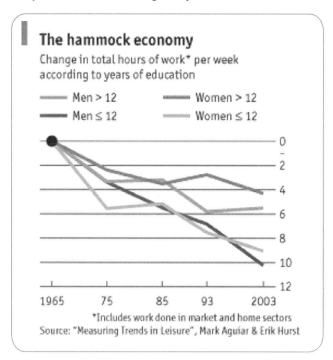

The hammock economy

Change in total hours of work* per week
according to years of education

— Men > 12   — Women > 12
— Men ≤ 12   — Women ≤ 12

0
2
4
6
8
10
12

1965   75   85   93   2003

*Includes work done in market and home sectors
Source: "Measuring Trends in Leisure", Mark Aguiar & Erik Hurst

AS MOST Americans will tell you, working people in the United States are as busy as ever. Sure, technology and competition are boosting the economy; but nearly everyone thinks they have increased the demands on people at home and in the workplace.

But is the overworked American a creature of myth?

Two economists have looked closely at how Americans actually spend their time. Mark Aguiar and Erik Hurst studied lots of American people's lives to see how much 'leisure time' they really had.

The results showed Americans seem to have much more free time than before.

● Over the past four decades the amount of time that working-age Americans are devoting to leisure activities has risen by 4-8 hours a week. (For somebody working 40 hours a week, that is equivalent to 5-10 weeks of extra holiday a year.)

- Nearly every category of American has more spare time: single or married, with or without children, both men and women. The only twist is that less educated (and thus poorer) Americans have done relatively better than more educated ones (see chart). And that is not just because unemployed high-school drop-outs have more free time on their hands. Less educated Americans with jobs do very well.

Some Americans won't believe these findings simply because they feel over-worked, and it is true that official statistics show many Americans put in longer hours at the office than other countries, but that is because average hours in the workplace in other rich countries have dropped sharply. In America, official studies tend to show women working more and men less, but the average working week has been fairly constant.

So how did Aguiar and Hurst come to such a different conclusion? The reasons are partly to do with the definition of work, and partly to do with the data they base their research upon.

Most American labor studies concentrate on paid work. These are good at identifying trends in factories and offices, but don't cover how Americans use the rest of their time.

Aguiar and Hurst think that the hours spent at your paid job equal only part of your actual 'work', and the time you spend shopping, cooking, running errands and keeping house should be counted too. But ....

Aguiar and Hurst show that Americans actually spend much less time doing them than they did 40 years ago. There has been a revolution in the household economy. Appliances, home delivery, the internet, 24-hour shopping, and so on have increased flexibility and freed up people's time.

So women are devoting more hours to paying jobs, but have cut their housework and other burdensome tasks by twice as much. Men have picked up some of the slack at home; but thanks to technology and other advances, there is plenty of free time left over for them as well, since they have yielded some of their paid working hours to women.

The data for Aguiar and Hurst's study comes from diaries that American social scientists have been collecting once a decade, since 1965. These diaries ask people to give detailed information on everything they did the day before, and for how long they did it.

Still, there are some problems with this data.

For example: they don't include retired people, who often have a lot of leisure time and money to spend on it. (Which means the leisure time numbers should be even higher.)

So why do Americans feel so busy and time starved?

One reason is that economic advances allow people to squeeze ever more possible activities, both work and leisure, into a day, which encourages people to try to do too much.
Another is the changing nature of work. Mobile phones and e-mail make people accountable on short notice, and competition may make them less secure in their jobs. So even if they are playing golf or walking in the park, they may feel as if they are working. It is surely nicer to feel overworked in the park than to be overworked at the office, but few Americans seem to look at it that way.

(Source: http://www.economist.com/node/5476124)

Reading Comprehension for Reading 1

TRUE or FALSE?

1. According to the research featured in the article most Americans have more leisure time now than ever before. T/F

2. Across the board - men and women, old and young, rich and poor all have more leisure time than ever. T/F

3. Aguiar and Hurst say this is due to a reduction of working hours. T/F

4. This research is based on data from Internet blogs. T/F

5. If the researchers had studied retired people the numbers would be higher. T/F

DISCUSSION

Your leisure time

Think about your average week, and note how many hours you spend:

- in school

- at work

- studying (not in class)

- commuting

- on personal grooming

- on chores

- eating

- sleeping

1. How much free time do you have left?

2. What do you do with it?

3. How much of it is spent on leisure activities?

4. What are they?

INTRODUCTION

Before you read

- Which jobs are the most common in your country?
- Can you quess the top five most common jobs in the USA/UK?
- What are some unusual jobs in the USA/UK?

When meeting someone for the first time in the UK or the US one of the first questions people ask each other is "What do you do?"

Our job is one of the main ways we establish social position and importance in the west. In general some jobs carry more status than others, ex: a doctor, or present a glamorous image, ex: model, photographer.

Higher paid jobs tend to attract more value than lower paid jobs, though this may depend on the situation. (For example, in an area with high unemployment having any job may be a major status symbol).

Last Coal Miners at Tower Colliery, UK

Questions to think about

1. How many years of your life do you think you will 'work'?

2. How many jobs do you think you will have?

3. Are JOBS in your country different from JOBS in the UK or USA?

4. Which jobs in your country need English skills?

RESEARCH

Which jobs are the most popular in your country? Which jobs in your country have the highest and lowest status?

- salary prospects?
- status?

Why is this so?

In most cultures the jobs with the highest status/pay often involve:

- extensive periods of study or training
- not getting dirty

Of course the opposite is usually true for work with the lowest status and pay.

- **Can you think of any new jobs these may be in the future?**

Look up "Sean Aiken". The man with 52 jobs!

- **Do you have a dream job in mind for when you graduate college?**

- **If you could do any job in the word what would it be?**

READING 1

Most Popular Jobs in America - Business Insider

OCCUPATIONAL EMPLOYMENT AND WAGES — MAY 2014

The Bureau of Labor Statistics has published a new report showing the top 10 most common professions in the U.S.

The top three are all basically in the retail industry: salespeople, cashiers, and fast-food workers.

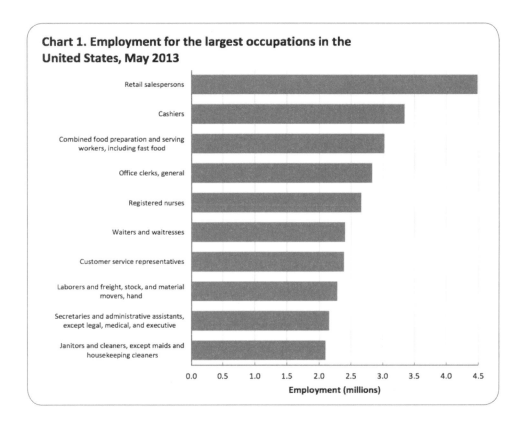

From May 2014 statistics retail salespersons and cashiers together made up nearly 6 percent of total U.S. employment, with employment levels of 4.6 million and 3.4 million, respectively.

The average wage in the USA is $47,230.

Of the 10 largest occupations, only registered nurses, with an annual mean wage of $69,790, had an above average wage.

The highest paying occupations overall included several physician and dentist occupations, chief executives, nurse anesthetists, and petroleum engineers.

Occupations

The 10 largest occupations accounted for 21 percent of total employment in May 2014. In addition to retail salespersons and cashiers, the largest occupations included combined food preparation and serving workers, including fast food; general office clerks; registered nurses; customer service representatives; and waiters and waitresses. (See chart 1.)

Most of the largest occupations were relatively low paying. Excluding registered nurses, annual mean wages for the rest of the 10 largest occupations ranged from $19,110 for combined food preparation and serving workers to $34,500 for secretaries and administrative assistants, except legal, medical, and executive.

Combined food preparation and serving workers also was one of the lowest paying occupations overall, along with fast food cooks ($19,030), shampooers ($19,480), and dishwashers ($19,540). (See chart 2.)

There were over 8.3 million STEM (Science, Technology, Engineering, Math) jobs in May 2014, representing about 6.2 percent of total U.S. employment. Seven of the 10 largest STEM occupations were related to computers.

These occupations included:

- applications software developers (686,470)
- computer user support specialists (563,540)
- computer systems analysts (528,320).

Wholesale and manufacturing sales representatives of technical and scientific products (335,540) was the largest STEM occupation that was not specifically computer related.
Ninety-three of the 100 STEM occupations had mean wages significantly above the average.

Of the top 10 jobs, nearly all are "low paying" work, with the exception of registered nurses.

This chart shows how they compare to the average.

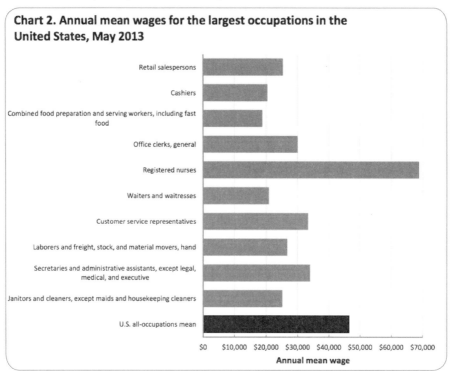

Occupational profiles for all occupations are available at www.bls.gov/oes/current/oes_stru.htm.

(Adapted from: http://www.businessinsider.com/most-popular-jobs-in-america-2014-4)

Activity 1 – Reading Comprehension

Match the first half of sentences from 1 - 8 with the correct second half from A - H

1	The three most common jobs in the USA
2	All but one of the most common jobs
3	Of all the STEM jobs in the USA
4	If you choose to work in a STEM occupation in the US
5	If you combine the salary of every working US citizen and divide this total by the total number of workers
6	People who work in restaurants
7	Registered nurses
8	Doctors, dentists and CEOs are

A	are generally the worst paid of all.
B	some of the best paying professions in the US.
C	are the only group in the top ten most common jobs who earn more than the national average.
D	you will get the average salary figure used to make comparisons across the board.
E	pay low salaries.
F	involve handling cash and providing good customer service.
G	the best paid involve computing.
H	you have a 93% chance of earning a lot more than the average person.

UK employment

In the UK jobs are usually broken down into these broad categories.

Category	Training	Pay	Examples
Professional/ Managerial	Undergrad or graduate degree Training	Usually salaried	Doctor Pilot Teacher
White collar	Usually studies for relevant qualification	Usually salaried	Bank worker, real estate agent, stockbroker

Blue collar (skilled)	Hands-on work, with training	Often salaried	Miner, lab tech, firefighter, police officer
Blue collar - unskilled	Manual labor, unlikely to need certain qualifications	Generally hourly paid or on a contract	Construction laborer, taxi driver, janitorial staff
Pink collar	Service industries	Varies from salary, or hourly to tips only	Maids, bar staff, wait staff, sales clerks,
Trades	Must take a 3-4 year apprenticeship course	Salaried, low while training. Later may be self employed or hourly paid too.	Car mechanic, plumber, carpenter etc

In the UK it is now considered normal to change careers several times during your lifetime.

How much holiday/vacation time do people get on average in your country?

Is it normal to have national (bank) holidays off work?

If yes, are these paid or unpaid?

If you work do you get extra money?

Activity 2 – QUIZ on UK employment

Work with a partner to answer these questions

1. In the UK the law says that anyone working full time (5 days/37 hours) must have at least:

   a) 5 ½ weeks   b) 3 ½ weeks   c) 10 weeks

2. In the UK men and women must be paid the same salary for doing the same job. This law was introduced in:

   a) 2000   b) 1970   c) 1980

3. In the UK, what % of people are self employed?

   a) 4%   b) 14%   c) 24%

4. The % of 16-18 year olds in the UK who have a Saturday job while at school or college is:

   a) 3%   b) 17%   c) 20%

INNOVATION

INTRODUCTION

What is innovation?

How do you listen to music?

> Records ▶ Tapes ▶ CDs ▶ MP3 ▶ Streaming

How do you communicate with your friends?

> Letters, Post Cards ▶ Telephones ▶ Pagers ▶ Mobile Phones ▶ Texting ▶ SNS

Do you know some of the most popular texting abbreviations?

Abbreviation	Meaning
gtg	got to go
lol	laugh out loud
rofl	roll on the floor laughing
l8r	later
b4	before
fyi	for your information
btw	by the way
asap	as soon as possible
cye	check your email
sup	what's up?
w/	with
brb	be right back
ttyl	talk to you later
xoxo	hugs and kisses

How has technology changed the culture and our lives?

How will 3D printers change the future?

Showing how to use the 3D printer

READING 1

Before you read

Decide if you agree or disagree with the following statements, then compare your answers with another student or the class, (depending on what your teacher tells you to do).

1. I read news reports via the Internet on my phone.	Agree/Disagree
2. If the page (or link) doesn't load within 10 seconds I close it.	Agree/Disagree
3. I read interesting websites via my phone.	Agree/Disagree
4. If the page (or link) doesn't load within 10 seconds I close it.	Agree/Disagree
5. I use social media e.g. Twitter or Facebook via my phone.	Agree/Disagree
6. If the page (or link) doesn't load within 10 seconds I close it.	Agree/Disagree
7. I prefer using mobile apps to the Internet, on my phone.	Agree/Disagree

If you 'agreed' with 5 or more you are the perfect target audience for what you will read about below.

Pre-reading – important vocabulary

digital magazine pieces – articles on online gossip, review and discussion sites
universal standard – the same level around the world
projected spend – the amount of money something will cost
cleanly formatted – look good on a small screen
the web feels clunky – hard to navigate
the undisputed king – everyone agrees they re top person or company
sway - influence
referral traffic to publishers – where people click to get to article

Google, Twitter and Publishers Seek Faster Web

In a world where many people read everything on mobile phones, a few extra seconds of load time can mean the loss of millions of readers, and of advertising dollars. Now Google wants to help publishers (and itself) by speeding things up.

Google is working with the social media service Twitter, and major news publishers like The New York Times, to create a new kind of web link and article storage system that would load online news articles and **digital magazine pieces** in a few milliseconds. That is a fraction of the five to 10 seconds it can take to load a typical website.

The project is still in its early stages, and the details are neither final or being made public yet, so this report depends on insider information.

The goal is to develop a **universal standard** for publishers - one that could be used to load articles faster, wherever they appear. But making this happen without changing how a page looks is not easy.

This new idea would also help stop Facebook and Apple keeping customers on their own sites, using apps instead of Google to find information.

Google makes most of its money from ads sold on websites, including its own search page. While Twitter, which depends on conversations around news articles for its traffic, wants to keep visitors on its platform longer.

Right now, (September 2015), neither Twitter and Google will talk about this project, or the pre-Christmas testing period that is planned.

The more time people spend with mobile devices, the less they use the web. This year, smartphone users in the United States are **projected to spend** 81% of their time using mobile apps, versus 19% using the mobile web.

People often favor mobile apps because they are faster, **cleanly formatted** and are constantly updated to take advantage of the evolving features of new smartphones.

Despite the migration to apps, much of the content inside popular services like Facebook, Twitter and Pinterest continues to come from web links, but compared to many modern apps **the web feels clunky** and slow, adding seconds of load time that can prompt impatient mobile users to move on to something else.

Google may still be **the undisputed king** of web search, but Facebook is starting to have more **sway** over publishers. In July, Facebook just beat Google for the share of referral traffic to publishers — about 40%, versus 38 percent for Google. Just two years ago Facebook only drove about 12 percent of **referral traffic to publishers**.

(Adapted from: http://www.nytimes.com/2015/09/12/technology/google-twitter-and-publishers-seek-faster-web.html)

Comprehension Questions

Read the article again, and make some notes to help you answer these questions;

1. Why do Google want to change the way websites load to mobile phones?

2. Who are Google working with to achieve this?

3. Why do Google want people to not use Facebook or Apple apps to find information?

4. Currently, what percentage of USA phone users choose mobile apps over the mobile web to find information?

5. Why do people prefer mobile apps?

ACTIVITY 1

Interested in Robots?

Do you have a robot vacuum cleaner?

Are robots becoming more like humans?

1. Before you watch the TED Talk, read this excerpt from the first part of Breazeal's talk. Which words do you think are missing? Complete each gap and share your ideas with a partner.

    a. delight   b. exist   c. explore   d. interacted

Ever since I was a little girl seeing Star Wars for the first time, I've been fascinated by this idea of personal robots. And as a little girl, I loved the idea of a robot that ① _____ with us much more like a helpful, trusted sidekick-something that would ② _____ us, enrich our like, and help us save a galaxy or two. I knew robots like that didn't really ③ _____, but I knew I wanted to build them.

So over the past several years, I've been continuing to ④ _____ this interpersonal dimension of robots, not at the Media Lab with my own team of incredibly talented students. And one of my favorite robots is in Leonardo.

> **Helpful Vocabulary**
>
> **Sidekick**: n. a close friend or helper
> **Enrich**: v. add good things to
> **Galaxy**: n. a large system of stars
> **Dimension**: n. an aspect or feature of something

2. Watch the TED Talk called "The rise of personal robots" by Cynthia Breazeal.

http://www.ted.com/talks/cynthia_breazeal_the_rise_of_personal_robots

3. Which statement best describes the main idea of this segment of the TED Talk?

    a. You cannot create a robot like Leonardo without a large team of incredibly talented people.

    b. If we build robots that communicate with us the way people do, they might be able to improve our lives.

    c. We need to establish labs where we can create robots like the ones we see in movies like Star Wars.

Breazeal with the robot Leonardo

4. Breazeal shows a demonstration of how Leonardo works. Number the steps of the demonstration in the correct order, from 1 to 7

    _____ Leo looks afraid.

    _____ Leo points to Cookie Monster.

    _____ Leo looks at Cookie Monster and nods his head.

    _____ Matt says "Hello" to Leo. Leo "hears" Matt and nods his head.

    _____ Matt tells Leo that Cookie Monster is very bad.

    _____ Matt asks Leo, "Can you find Cookie Monster?"

    _____ Matt shows Leo a puppet called "Cookie Monster."

(Source: 21st Century Reading 1, Cengage Learning)

READING 2

Before you read

'The Martian' Shows 9 Ways NASA Tech Is Headed to Mars

In the sci-fi film "The Martian," astronaut Mark Watney (played by Matt Damon) is stranded on Mars. He is alone and thought to be dead.

Watney must figure out a way to survive on the inhospitable planet, and somehow alert NASA that he is still alive so they can try to rescue him. As he is an engineer he can adapt technology to fit his needs.

How much of the technology Watney uses actually exists today, or should exist in the near future? Read on to learn about the tech NASA is developing as part of its effort to put humans on Mars in the 2030s.

1. Humans on Mars
In "The Martian," Watney uses pieces of his immediate environment to make the new items he needs. He can also stay safe inside his living space.

NASA hasn't built a real Mars habitat yet, but the agency has created a fake one in Houston, Texas. Astronauts currently stay there for 14 days, on pretend missions. This will become 60 days at some point in the future.

2. A Mars Farm
Watney needs food to eat on Mars so he tries to grow a lot of potatoes in his habitat.

In space, astronauts are starting to grow crops of their own. For example, astronauts aboard the International Space Station recently harvested the first lettuce leaves from the "Veggie" experiment, which is intended to help NASA learn how to establish and maintain off-Earth farms.

3. Water recovery
Watney has problems trying to save water on Mars.

This same challenge confronts astronauts on the International Space Station, who recycle their urine and sweat for drinking water and other purposes.

4. Oxygen generation
Watney gets oxygen on Mars using a system called the "oxygenator," which creates oxygen from the carbon dioxide used in his fuel generator.

Astronauts aboard the space station use an oxygen-generation system that splits water molecules into hydrogen and oxygen. The oxygen flows into the atmosphere for breathing, while some of the hydrogen is used for water.

5. Mars spacesuit
Watney spends much of his time on Mars in a spacesuit, repairing his habitat and performing some long-distance treks.

NASA is working on some real spacesuit technologies that could be used on Mars, such as the Z-2 and Prototype exploration Suit. Astronauts climb into these suits from the rear, so they can leave the suits outside their Mars habitats, reducing dust entry.

6. Mars rover
Watney's rover on Mars is designed to perform short trips but he makes several changes to it so he can travel much further.

NASA is creating a six-wheeled Multi-Mission Space Exploration Vehicle (MMSEV) that will do the same. If it gets a flat tire it just lifts that wheel up and continues on the other five wheels!!

(Adapted from: http://www.space.com/30360-the-martian-movie-nasa-mars-technology.html)

● You may research more about NASA and/or SpaceX.

SpaceX Falcon 9 rocket, USA

Note:

Ranking Activity

Follow the instruction your teacher gives you.

LIST 1

1.
2.
3.
4.
5.
6.
7.
8.
9.
10.

LIST 2

1.
2.
3.
4.
5.

LIST 3

1.
2.
3.
4.
5.

LIST 4

1.
2.
3.

Answer Key

(instructions for some activities included)

Chapter 1: Introduction

Vocabulary Activity for Reading

a -3   b - 5   c - 1   d - 6   e - 4   f - 2   g - 7

Reading Comprehension

The author:

1. Thinks Korea is becoming a more multicultural society.   T
2. Claims that non-Koreans have less rights than Korean citizens.   T
3. Believes (Asian) foreign wives are rarely considered full citizens. T
4. Says that the influence of Confucianism stops Korea developing fully.   T
5. Thinks Korean society has not prepared itself for the changes a multicultural society needs to make. T

Chapter 2: Language

Activity 1

Student 1	Student 2
Give you a bell b) Call you	Wonky c) Not right or uneven
Gutted a) Devastated (very disappointed)	Skive b) Avoid doing something
Chuffed b) Proud	Toff b) Upper class
Lost the Plot a) Gone Crazy	Starkers a) Naked
Sorted c) Arranged	Loo b)Toilet
Kip b) Sleep or nap	Nicked c) Stolen
Bee's Knees a) Awesome	Gobsmacked c) Amazed
Dodgy c) Suspicious	Bog Roll a) Toilet Paper

Activity 2

Korean	British English	American English
1. 승강기	Lift	Elevator
2. 우편	Post	Mail
3. 감자칩	Chips	Fries
4. 감자튀김	Crisps	Chips
5. 반창고	Plasters	Band aid
6. 운동화	Trainers	Sneakers
7. 쿠키	Biscuits	Cookies
8. 약국	Chemist's shop	Pharmacy/Drug store
9. 축구	Football	Soccer
10. 미식축구	American football	Football
11. 트렁크	Boot (of car)	Trunk (of car)
12. 스웨터	Jumper	Sweater
13. 기름(차량용)	Petrol	Gas
14. 주차장	Car park	Parking
15. 핸드폰	Mobile phone	Cell phone (영국 ok)
16. 지하철	Under ground, Tube	Subway
17. 인도	Pavement	Sidewalk
18. 1층	Ground floor, Lobby	First floor
19. 손전등	Torch	Flash light
20. 아파트	Flat	Apartment
21. 사탕	Sweets	Candy
22. 가을	Autumn	Fall
23. 술집	Pub	Bar
24. 쓰레기통	Bin	Trash Can
25. 냅킨	Serviette	Napkin

Chapter 3: Family

T/F Activity on Facts

1. True
2. True
3. False - 1.9 on average
4. True
5. True

Reading 1 (gapfill)

modest
recession
multi-generational households
splits the phone bill
pitching in
friction

Comprehension Questions for Reading 1

1. Tam is used to it. She spends most of her time at her parent's house so eventually she decided to move in.
2. 5 adults
3. adantages: share chores
   disadvantages: little privacy

Reading 2
Exercise 2
Match the words and definitions, then compare your answers with someone else in your class.

LIST A	LIST B
Eldest	Stop doing something
Important milestones	Badly organized/too casual/careless
Quit	A person who buys, improves and sells buildings
Flick through	A big event in your life e.g. baby learns to talk
Sloppy	Look through something
Commercial property developer	The oldest

Exercise 3

What do these numbers refer to?

39 (Katie's age now)

18 months (her youngest child)

7 (number of girls she has)

3 (age of her twins)

1999 (year had first baby)

11 months (age of first baby when she went back to paid work)

One and a half days (time nanny works with them)

Check your Understanding for Reading 2

1. a
2. b
3. b

Chapter 4: Celebrations

Comprehension questions for Reading 2

1. 17th March
2. Roman Britain, 4th century
3. Irish pirates
4. No
5. Green
6. Own answers

Chapter 5: Houses

Comprehension Questions for Reading 2
"Ana Finds an Apartment"

1) D
2) C

3) D
4) D
5) D
6) A
7) C
8) A
9) B
10) C
11) C
12) D

Jigsaw Activity for Reading 2

You need to prepare sticky notes or paper squares. Example: if you have 15 students you need:

- **five papers with number 1 on**
- **five papers with the number 2 on**
- **five papers with number 3 on**

1. Organize the students into three groups or around the same size. Give each student on one group the SAME number/letter (??) reading and a few minutes to read it. Make sure that they a) read ONLY their section and b) make the effort to identify and remember the key facts. They can check any words or discuss the reading only with their group.

2. Use the squares of paper or sticky notes you have prepared here. Give ALL the students:
   - in group A/1 a paper with 1 on it
   - in group B/2 a paper with 2 on it
   - in group C/3 a paper with 3 on it

3. Have them make new groups - each should have a student with a number 1, 2 and 3 paper. (There will probably be a couple of extra people, they can join any other groups to make a 4.)

4. Now the students must share what they remember from their own section of the story with their small group. **They are not allowed to look at the reading again, or any notes they have made.**

If it is possible you can extend this activity and have them produce something (a play or drama, song, picture etc) based on the shared knowledge.

British and American Food Words

9	Aubergine
5	Courgette
2	Biscuit
4	Chips
10	Chocolate bar
8	Crisps
1	Fizzy drink
3	Ice lolly
7	Porridge
6	Sweets

Reading 1 (Version A) - What is British Food?

1. heavy, greasy ,bland
2. Vikings
3. Bangers
4. Lunchtime

Reading 1 (Version B) - What is British Food?

1. fish and chips
2. mashed potato
3. Sunday
4. 5-6

Comprehension questions for Reading 2

1 - b
2 - a
3 - d
4 – c or d
5 – d

Extension: Design your ideal school weekly timetable

Chapter 8 Leisure

Activity 1 - Introduction to UK Leisure

arts & entertainment

parks & open spaces

sports clubs & fitness

events

beaches

museums & local history

leisure projects

libraries

tourism & travel

parks & open spaces

Activity 2
Match the vocabulary and definitions

1	2	3	4	5
d	b	e	i	c
6	7	8	9	10
a	g	h	j	f

Comprehension Task

1. Most people in the UK are involved either actively or passively in recreational pursuits.
2. More people are engaging in keep fit activities than in the past
3. You can do sport inside or outside or free or pay to join a sports club.
4. Many free time activities are less strenuous in nature.
5. Most urban areas will have something to suit you, irrespective of age.

Reading Comprehension for Reading 1

TRUE or FALSE?

1. According to the research featured in the article most Americans have more leisure time now than ever before. (True)
2. Across the board - men and women, old and young, rich and poor all have more leisure time than ever. (True)
3. Aguiar and Hurst say this is due to a reduction of working hours. (False)
4. This research is based on data from Internet blogs (False)
5. If the researchers had studied retired people the numbers would be higher. (True)

Chapter 9: Jobs

Activity 1- Answer Needed

1 – F
1 – E
1 – G
1 – H
1 – D
1 – A
1 – C
1 – B

Activity 2 - QUIZ

1 – a 5 ½ weeks
2 – b 1970
3 – b 14%
4 – c 20%

Reading 1: Google, Twitter and Publishers Seek Faster Web

Comprehension Questions

Read the article again, and make some notes to help you answer these questions;

1. Why do Google want to change the way websites load to mobile phones?
   They want people to follow links via Google rather thn through aps like \fb, as Google make cash from ads , which need viewers

2. Who are Google working with to achieve this?
   Twitter and the NY Times

3. Why do Google want people to not use Facebook or Apple apps to find information?
   It takes them away from the web browsers.

4. Currently, what percentage of USA phone users choose mobile apps over the mobile web to find information?
   81%

5. Why do people prefer mobile apps?
   They are faster.

Activity 1

① d
② a
③ b
④ c

Activity 2

Instructions for the teacher

1. Explain the following scenario – they (the entire class) will be going to live in a safe Mars habitat for one year. Basic food, water and clothing will be provided.
2. Have the students create an individual 'list 1' – 10 things they want to take with them.
3. Have the students make pairs and compare/discuss their choices. Together they must create 'list 2' – 5 items which they can agree on taking, these MUST come from their own 'list 1'. (If you have an uneven number it is okay to group 3 students together.)
4. Now arrange the students into groups of 3. Wherever possible these should be all new groups, so use a numbering system or just choose new groups for yourself. They will have 15 items between them, which they must break down to 5 – creating an agreed 'list 3'.
5. For 'list 4' create groups of 4 people (preferably mixing them all up again), so each new group should have 20 items to choose from. They need to agree on the final 3.
6. Write the final 3 choices from each group on the board and discuss the results.

Chapter 3. Family

Family word search

T	S	R	B	G	G	F	Q	C	D	R	S	Q	E	A	R	FAMILY
M	W	P	C	V	O	M	U	O	B	Q	T	G	Z	Z	I	DAD
B	N	S	C	C	O	W	F	S	C	X	E	G	T	S	Q	STEPFATHER
R	D	A	D	A	U	G	H	T	E	R	P	R	H	G	H	DAUGHTER
O	S	V	W	I	E	J	G	G	U	L	F	A	M	U	M	BROTHER
T	B	S	I	S	T	E	R	G	X	G	A	U	D	J	G	AUNT
H	V	M	F	B	V	P	A	I	X	C	T	N	G	B	R	COUSIN
E	R	O	U	O	R	T	N	F	B	I	H	T	F	M	A	GRANDFATHER
R	P	Y	I	F	O	J	D	K	A	G	E	K	L	L	N	MUM
F	C	W	X	A	F	O	M	Z	B	P	R	N	U	J	D	STEPMOTHER
B	O	P	V	M	E	P	O	U	Y	S	O	N	A	W	F	SON
J	U	D	T	I	E	K	T	N	Z	V	E	P	E	S	A	BABY
K	S	D	W	L	D	M	H	C	D	E	F	Z	S	R	T	SISTER
C	I	G	J	Y	K	R	E	L	A	T	I	V	E	S	H	UNCLE
M	N	U	O	E	E	Q	R	E	M	Q	M	W	G	A	E	GRANDMOTHER
Y	E	B	D	S	T	E	P	M	O	T	H	E	R	K	R	RELATIVES

Can you find all the words in just 5 minutes?

Family idioms quiz

Work in a pair or team to decide on the most likely answer. You can check them on later pages.

In the family way means someone who:
a) lives with the family
b) does things the same way as the family
c) is pregnant

The black sheep of the family refers to a person who:
a) behaves in a way the family don't like
b) acts like an animal
c) works at a zoo

Keep it in the family means:
a) don't give food to non-family members
b) spend your free time with family
c) don't talk about something to non-family members

Activity 1 - *Tell an alien about …. a special day*

Imagine that you have to explain a popular holiday that is special to your country to an alien! Work with a partner or small group to work out what you would say. Use the worksheet **below** to help guide you and keep a record of your work to share with others.

Holiday chosen	
When is it?	
Why is it important?	
What happens?	
Preparation?	
Food	
Clothes	

Share your ideas with the class

Activity 2 – *Thinking up a new holiday*

Work with a partner or a small group to think of a new holiday to celebrate in your country. It could be serious or funny, or draw attention to something you think is important. Use the worksheet prompts to make notes. If you have time share your idea with another group.

Type of holiday	(Legal, cultural, personal)
Name	
Date	
What it celebrates	
Who is it aimed at?	
Important rituals	
Special food	
Anything else	

Share your ideas with the class

Fun Quiz

1. How many donuts are made/sold/eaten in the USA every year?

   10 billion   5 billion   30 million

2. What percentage (%) of meals do Americans eat in their car?

   50%   10%   20%

3. Which popular soft drink was first sold as a kind of medicine?

   Coca Cola   Fanta   Pepsi   Sprite

Food Idioms

Use the words in the list below to complete the sentences.

1. It's a piece of _____.
2. They are like chalk and _____.
3. Stop _____ me up.
4. Don't spill the _____.
5. Bring home the _____.
6. You are the _____ of my eye.
7. Don't put all your _____ in one basket.
8. It's not my cup of _____.

| cheese |
| cake |
| bacon |
| buttering |
| tea |
| apple |
| eggs |
| beans |

(Made via www.TheTeachersCorner.net)

Let's be food detectives

Watch a video showing the food people eat around the world. Can you identify any differences between different regions of the world?

TEACHER TIP: Here is one example

https://www.youtube.com/watch?v=uJEsM-ep7EQ

If it is not available try searching for 'food eaten in a week around the world'

Remember that what you see doesn't necessarily represent everyone in a country.

After watching

In the introduction to this topic there is a list of clues that food gives us about a person's life, including where they live, their class, and sometimes also their religion and ethnic background.

Can you remember anything from the food featured video that told you about each person or family's lives? Make a few notes on what you remember below.

Now watch the video again. Your teacher may choose to pause on certain countries or play the entire thing. Can you add anything to your notes above?

Share your ideas with your classmates and teacher. How did you come to these answers? How do you know they are accurate?

Extension Activity

Chose one country featured in the video and research the average spend on food, typical diet, and any cultural or religious restrictions on diet.

Match the picture and food

Apple pie A popular dessert in the UK. • •	
Traditional British breakfast Sausage, bacon, beans, tomatoes, mushrooms, eggs, black pudding and toast. • •	
Pancakes/hotcakes An American favorite. • •	
Tacos Popular in the USA. The orginal recioe is Mexican. • •	
Soul food Traditional food in the southern states of the USA. • •	
Fish and chips One of the UKs favourite take out meals. • •	

Opinion Activity

Quiz on table manners, etiquette, traditions. What is considered rude in the US, UK and in your country? Mark with a circle if you think something is rude behavior.

		USA	UK	Your country
1	Eating with only a fork			
2	Speaking with your mouth full			
3	Putting salt on food before you taste it			
4	Making noises* while eating			
	*(ex: slurping, smacking lips, groans of pleasure)			
5	Talking at the dinner table			
6	Eating before everyone has been served			
7	Taking food from someone's plate without being invited to			

DISCUSSION: compare results with your group members, and add more ideas from your culture on what is polite and impolite.

Teacher Tip – a good extension activity would be either a research project, or an information gathering task to prepare for a debate, on topics such as:
* food banks vs food waste
* obesity vs the malnourished

Or perhaps have them create a poster explaining the differences between a vegetarian, vegan, fruitarian and pescatarian

Can you find all 15 jobs? Remember to strike through each word on the list when you find it.
(Each letter can only be used once.)

```
Z  R  I  S  D  X  T  U  R  O  S  R  R  L  A
D  Q  O  T  A  S  A  E  D  T  V  E  E  R  A
E  A  B  T  I  L  T  D  O  Z  R  H  T  E  Y
F  V  I  R  C  R  E  R  X  E  F  P  H  S  I
T  K  O  R  O  U  E  S  T  B  Y  A  G  I  Z
R  L  G  P  Y  K  R  S  M  O  B  R  I  A  U
F  Z  E  H  E  F  A  T  B  A  G  G  F  R  H
N  R  B  E  C  M  A  W  S  R  N  O  E  D  U
B  R  P  G  W  I  O  R  W  N  H  T  R  N  S
I  E  Z  E  D  C  Y  M  M  G  I  O  I  U  L
R  X  R  B  A  K  E  R  F  E  M  H  F  F  Q
W  B  A  F  P  I  L  O  T  X  R  P  V  F  W
R  O  T  A  R  T  S  N  O  M  E  D  X  H  N
T  A  L  K  S  H  O  W  H  O  S  T  X  X  E
P  I  Z  Z  A  M  A  K  E  R  Q  Q  W  Z  F
```

BAKER	BREWMASTER
COWBOY	DAIRYFARMER
DEMONSTRATOR	FIREFIGHTER
FLORIST	FUNDRAISER
INSTRUCTOR	PHOTOGRAPHER
PILOT	PIZZAMAKER
REPORTER	SALESMAN
STOREKEEPER	TALKSHOWHOST

(http://puzzlemaker.discoveryeducation.com/)

Sean Aiken. The man with 52 jobs!

Do you have a dream job in mind for when you graduate college?

If you could do any job in the word what would it be?

Sean Aiken is an Australian who kept hearing people say they needed passion for their work. He didn't know what kind of job made him feel that way so he decided to try a few out, one per week, 52 jobs in one year!

Watch the video trailer for a show about him here: http://www.oneweekjob.com/
Episodes from his show are also available here: http://www.oneweekjob.com/about-the-project/previous-jobs/
Would you like to try something like this? Why, or why not?

Optional Task (in class or at home)

Choose one of his videos and watch it.
Identify the job he did, what it involved, his good and bad experiences, and if he found his passion.

Your teacher may ask you to present, share or post your results somewhere.

Answers for Additional Activites

Chapter 3. Family

Family members word search solution

T	S	R	B	G	G	F	Q	C	D	R	S	Q	E	A	R
M	W	P	C	V	O	M	U	O	B	Q	T	G	Z	Z	I
B	N	S	C	C	O	W	F	S	C	X	E	G	T	S	Q
R	D	A	D	A	U	G	H	T	E	R	P	R	H	G	H
O	S	V	W	I	E	J	G	G	U	L	F	A	M	U	M
T	B	S	I	S	T	E	R	G	X	G	A	U	D	J	G
H	V	M	F	B	V	P	A	I	X	C	T	N	G	B	R
E	R	O	U	O	R	T	N	F	B	I	H	T	F	M	A
R	P	Y	I	F	O	J	D	K	A	G	E	K	L	L	N
F	C	W	X	A	F	O	M	Z	B	P	R	N	U	J	D
B	O	P	V	M	E	P	O	U	Y	S	O	N	A	W	F
J	U	D	T	I	E	K	T	N	Z	V	E	P	E	S	A
K	S	D	W	L	D	M	H	C	D	E	F	Z	S	R	T
C	I	G	J	Y	K	R	E	L	A	T	I	V	E	S	H
M	N	U	O	E	E	Q	R	E	M	Q	M	W	G	A	E
Y	E	B	D	S	T	E	P	M	O	T	H	E	R	K	R

FAMILY   MUM

DAD   STEPMOTHER

STEPFATHER   SON

DAUGHTER   BABY

BROTHER   SISTER

AUNT   UNCLE

COUSIN   GRANDMOTHER

GRANDFATHER   RELATIVES

Idioms quiz

In the family way means someone who: c
   a) lives with the family
   b) does things the same way as the family
   c) is pregnant

The black sheep of the family refers to a person who: a
   a) behaves in a way the family don't like
   b) acts like an animal
   c) works at a zoo

Keep it in the family means: c
   a) don't give food to non-family members
   b) spend your free time with family
   c) don't talk about something to non-family members

Fun Quiz

1. How many donuts are made/sold/eaten in the USA every year? **10 billion**
2. What percentage (%) of meals do Americans eat in their car? **20%**
3. Which popular soft drink was first sold as a kind of medicine? **Coca Cola**

Food idioms

1. It's a piece of <u>cake</u>.
2. They are like chalk and <u>cheese</u>.
3. Stop <u>buttering</u> me up.
4. Don't spill the <u>beans</u>.
5. Bring home the <u>bacon</u>.
6. You are the <u>apple</u> of my eye.
7. Don't put all your <u>eggs</u> in one basket.
8. It's not my cup of <u>tea</u>.

Opinion Activity

	USA	UK
1	No problem unless at a formal dinner	Considered either rude or odd, although it is becoming more popular
2	Rude	Rude
3	Rude	Rude
4	Rude	Rude/odd
5	Regular conversation is no problem, (except for some very old fashioned/ traditional families) but it is generally rude to dominate the chat or to mention sensitive s ubjects which people may not agree on (ex: religion, politics)	Same as USA
6	Not polite when a meal is being served 'family style (dishes passed from person to person to serve themselves>)	Rude in a formal situation (at a dinner table or in a restaurant) unless invited to go ahead and start.
7	Rude	Rude

Answer key

```
+  R  +  S  +  +  T  +  R  +  S  R  R  +  +
D  +  O  +  A  S  +  E  +  T  +  E  E  R  +
+  A  +  T  I  L  T  +  O  +  R  H  T  E  +
+  +  I  R  C  R  E  R  +  E  +  P  H  S  +
+  +  O  R  O  U  E  S  T  +  Y  A  G  I  +
+  L  +  P  Y  K  R  S  M  O  +  R  I  A  +
F  +  E  +  E  F  A  T  B  A  +  G  F  R  +
+  R  +  E  +  M  A  W  S  +  N  O  E  D  +
+  +  P  +  W  +  O  R  +  N  +  T  R  N  +
+  E  +  E  +  C  +  +  M  +  I  O  I  U  +
R  +  R  B  A  K  E  R  +  E  +  H  F  F  +
+  B  +  +  P  I  L  O  T  +  R  P  +  +  +
R  O  T  A  R  T  S  N  O  M  E  D  +  +  +
T  A  L  K  S  H  O  W  H  O  S  T  +  +  +
P  I  Z  Z  A  M  A  K  E  R  +  +  +  +  +
```

(Over,Down,Direction)
BAKER(4,11,E)
BREWMASTER(2,12,NE)
COWBOY(6,10,NE)
DAIRYFARMER(1,2,SE)
DEMONSTRATOR(12,13,W)
FIREFIGHTER(13,11,N)
FLORIST(1,7,NE)
FUNDRAISER(14,11,N)
INSTRUCTOR(11,10,NW)
PHOTOGRAPHER(12,12,N)
PILOT(5,12,E)
PIZZAMAKER(1,15,E)
REPORTER(2,8,NE)
SALESMAN(4,1,SE)
STOREKEEPER(11,1,SW)
TALKSHOWHOST(1,14,E)

A Note for the Teacher

Here you will find tips, ideas and suggestions for things to supplement class work, or homework. There are both links and keywords for some topics, although links to online materials are likely to suddenly disappear, so please bear this in mind and prepare a back up source.

If you would like to get some more material, ask about anything covered or offer any feedback/suggestions for revised editions you can contact me (Val) at farawayhammer@gmail.com

Facebook

I have found Facebook to be a really useful teaching aid. If you would like to try it you can read more about how I used it here.

I create a new group for each class, then show the page with the group name on the screen in class. I create it through my personal FB page but make it clear to the students that I don't accept friend requests from them. However, if you prefer it may be easier to make a second account which you use just for work.

Once the class have joined the group I set it to secret, to avoid random requests to join.

On the Facebook page I use:

- the file section to upload supplementary class notes (useful for absent students)
- the events section to run 'make-up' classes needed due to school holidays or any unavoidable absence of my own
- the general page to post interesting facts and links, make announcements (which I pin for a while), and as a space for students to do extra work, which they can share and comment on between themselves
- the photo section to upload useful images

Video material

Try YouTube, Vimeo and Daily Motion, as well as anything random you come across in a web search.

Unit	Topic	Notes
1	**Introduction**	There is a lot of written and video based material online looking at 'rules' relating to pavements/sidewalks, bathrooms etc. The videos are always popular in class. **(As always though you should watch them first yourself, to make sure they are suitable for your class)** * **Here are a few leads:** Male restroom rules https://www.youtube.com/watch?v= IzO1mCAVy Mw Sidewalk rules https://www.youtube.com/watch?v=vgMnlGOw7wM Dining rules https://www.youtube.com/watch?v=HDTB7jsc0UY * For more on Maslow read: http://www.simplypsychology.org/maslow. html * This site has lots of good links and cool pictures http://www.michellehenry.fr/polite.htm
2	**Language**	Look online for sound bites of accents. Students could try to guess the country, even the region.
3	**Family**	**USEFUL LINKS** http://www.ons.gov.uk/ons/rel/family-demography/families-and-households/2014/families-and-households-in-the-uk--2014.html A higher level article about the way marriage and the family has changed over the centuries. http://theweek.com/articles/475141/how-marriage-changed-over-centuries Look online for 'Project Britain'. The site has lots of information on every aspect of culture covered in this book. YouTube, Vimeo and DailyMotion all have some good video material available. Though of course you should find and watch it before using in class. There are lots of TV shows/sitcom clips based around different family types available online
4	**Celebrations**	* Good topic for mid-term assignments/projects. * Look at Google images for 'painted Easter eggs' and 'chocolate Easter eggs') * Find video of UK pancake races.

5	**Houses**	* Can look at 'tiny homes' or social issues such as homelessness
		* Google weird houses around the world >>>> images
		(Ask: Which ones would you like to look inside/live in? Why?)
		* **Housing vocabulary** and discussion/research:
		http://www.esl-lab.com/vocab/v-housing.htm
		* **Architecture vocabulary**
		https://tefltastic.wordpress.com/worksheets/business-esp/architecture/
		architecture-adjectives/
		* **Secret pictures** - inside iconic buildings" http://www.dailymail.co.uk/
		news/article-2782769/Inside-London-s-hidden-architecture-Photographer-
		reveals-interior-secrets-iconic-buildings-including-Big-Ben-Bank-
		England.html
		* **World's top 20 iconic buildings (Lots of information on each**
		building - good watch at home activity)
		https://www.youtube.com/watch?v=DjYPWjjXj38
		* Top 10 iconic buildings: https://www.youtube.com/watch?v=
		4mzP7DGmo08
6	**Food**	Lots of culturally based video clips from TV shows.
		Can also think about food eating competitions.
		Info on breakfast: www.elcivics.com/lifeskills/breakfast-lesson-1.html
		Grocery shopping: www.elcivics.com/esl_grocery_shopping_1.html
		Puzzle link: www.elcivics.com/grocery_store_crossword_puzzle.pdf
		UK food: http://projectbritain.com/food/index.htm
		What I Eat: photographer Peter Menzel and writer Faith D'Aluisio present
		thought-provoking portraits of individuals around the globe and the food
		that fuels them over the course of a single day.
		www.time.com has some interesting photo galleries on this topic
		http://time.com/8515/hungry-planet-what-the-world-eats/ (photographs-
		27 countries)
		http://resources.woodlands-junior.kent.sch.uk/customs/food.html
		http://english.stackexchange.com/questions/22446/lunch-vs-dinner-vs-
		supper-times-and-meanings
		http://family.jrank.org/pages/639/Food-Food-Culture.html#ixzz3m5il0vkU
		Statistics (UK): https://www.gov.uk/government/uploads/system/uploads/
		attachment_data/file/461296/foodpocketbook-2015report-17sep15.pdf
7	**Education**	Article on how education is failing students: https://www.studentsfirst.org/
		pages/the-stats
		* Primary (Elementary) school http://projectbritain.com/education/index.
		html
		* Britain - this is school https://www.youtube.com/

		watch?v=yMUJKH1fFF0 * Uniforms (images) Google search 'UK school uniform' * Uniform (video) debate - good or bad? https://www.youtube.com/watch?v=dNvjAJTt2IM * School lunch around the world https://www.youtube.com/watch?v=Po0O9tRXCyA * UK secondary school lunches https://www.youtube.com/watch?v=Nt4iB96__YM
8	**Leisure**	Interesting links: * Strange British traditions https://www.youtube.com/watch?v=vu8C9qZHxXc * Weird sports https://www.youtube.com/watch?v=mN_8TN8pnjM * Wellie throwing https://www.youtube.com/watch?v=bqOcq0E-P-o http://resources.woodlands-junior.kent.sch.uk/customs/questions/weekends.htm http://resources.woodlands-junior.kent.sch.uk/customs/questions/sport.html
10	**Innovation**	Interesting links: TED talks of 2015 https://youtu.be/yWRmWnPNkqU Awesome Top New Technology https://youtu.be/VxwsBSoenqs

Finish with weekly task of each student writing on the small paper given (no names)

Things I have learned today:

Things I didn't understand today:

Questions I have about today:

About the Authors

김지나 (Gina Kim)

경력

Professor, Dept. of English Language and Literature, Hoseo University (S. Korea)
현 호서대학교 영어영문학과 교수 (2007-현재)

Admin Professor, CK-1 Project (Korean Ministry of Education) at Hoseo University
대학특성화사업 CK-1 호서대학교 외국어사업단 실무교수 (2014-2016)

Director, International Education Center for the Gifted, Hoseo University
전 호서대학교 국제영재교육원 원장 (2012-2015)

Vice-dean, International Exchange and Education, Hoseo University
전 호서대학교 국제협력원 부원장 (2012-2013)

Westpark Elementary School, ESL teacher.
전 미국, 웨스트마크 초등학교 ESL 교사 (1999)

Korean Representative, World Youth Leadership Training Summit, United Nations Headquarters, NY.
United Nations 50주년 기념 대표자 회의 한국대표 (1995)

Korean Representative, Lillehammer Winter Olympics Youth Commitee
Lillehammer 동계올림픽 청소년 리더십 한국대표 (1994)

학력

Hoseo University, Ph.D (S. Korea)
University of Idaho, M.A. (USA)
Aberdeen Grammar School (UK)

About the Authors

Valerie Hamer

경력

Professor, College of General Education, Hoseo University.
현 호서대학교 교양학부대학 교수 (2013-현재)

Lecturer, Durham University and in community education. (UK)
영국 더햄 대학 강사 (1994-2000)

TESOL teacher trainer, middle school and university lecturer. (Asia)
TESOL 교사 지도자, 중등-대학 강사, 아시아 (2000-2007)

15 years of experience teaching culture based classes.
Published two nonfiction books.
Presented papers on various aspects of culture at several conferences (UK)
Multi-cultural event planner for literary events.
Curriculum Manager for 'British Baking Club' for Asian students

학력

University of Lampeter, Wales, U.K. Social Anthropology M.A.
University of Falmouth, UK, Professional Writing M.A.
University of Cambridge, C.E.L.T.A.

References

강희봉, 박춘숙, 김수미, 김은실. 2012. High School Advanced English Reading II. 경기도교육청.

박의재, 황인태, 신두호. 2011. 미국과 영국의 사회와 문화. 서울: HSMEDIA .

이완기, 김진석, 장은숙. 2012. 문화 속의 영어 영어 속의 문화. 경기: 제이와이북스.

조일제. 2010. 영미문화의 이해와 탐방. 서울: 우용출판사

Dodd, H. D. 1997. Perspectives on cross-cultural communication. Iowa: Kendall-Hunt Publishing Company.

Gollnick, D. & Chinn, P. 2002. Multicultural Education in a Pluralistic Society(9th Ed.). NJ: Pearson.

Gooden, P. 2009. The Story of English. Glasgow: Quercus.

Longshaw, R. & Blass, L. 2015. 21st Century Reading, Student Book 1. Boston: National Geographic Learning/Cengage Learning.

Moore, E. 2015. That's not English. NY: Avery

Pesola, C. 1991. Culture in the elementary foreign language classroom. Foreign Language Annals, 24, 331-346.

Ting-Toomey, S. 1999. Communicating across cultures. London: The Guilford Press.

*Other sources are sited in the context

Additional Books that Helped

정동빈. 2008. 성공적인 영어교육을 위하여 정동빈 교수가 콕콕 짚어주는 영미문화 이해. 서울: 도서출판 동인.

태혜숙. 2009. 다인종 다문화 시대의 미국 문화 읽기. 도서출판 이후.

Banks, J. & Banks, C. 2009. Multicultural Education, Issues and Perspectives (7th Ed). NY: Wiley.

Collie, J. & Martin, A. 2000. What's It Like? Life and Culture in Britain Today. Cambridge: Cambridge University Press

Garwood, C., Gardini, G., & Peris, E. 1992. Aspects of Britain and the USA. Oxford: Oxford University Press.

Tomalin, B. & Stempleski, S. 1993. Cultural Awareness. Oxford: Oxford University Press.